FINALLY BACK
TO MY ROUTES

JOSIE DRAGE-DAWES

To Janet
Thank you oo much
for supporting me will
my Book
Joee X

J Drage-Dawes.

DEDICATION

This is dedicated to the ones I love
- The Mammas & Pappas

This book is dedicated to my daughter Ali

One of her last requests before she died was
'Mam, why don't you finish writing your book?'
That was twenty-five years ago this July
and now it's finally here.

CONTENTS

CHAPTER 1

The Early Days

I was born in a house at 10 Craigmuir Road, Ferguslie Park, (Feegie) Paisley on 17th August 1945. My maw was Mary McFarlane, and my father was George McKenna and apparently, I was one of fifteen children.

My only one memory of leaving Craigmuir Road was in 1951 when I was five or six years old. Most of the children living in the street - 'The Moor,' as it was known to us - were playing outside at the time. I was with my younger sister Louise, my older brother Eric with some other kids. We knew something was happening when these two big black taxis pulled into the road. Two women stepped out of one of them and walked up our close. Then myself, Louise and Gussie - my older sister aged 13, who was holding 18-month-old Frankie - were ushered into one of the taxis. We watched as the other woman came out of the close with another three of my older brothers, Rab, Tam, and Eric.

My father had died a year and a half earlier. The same day that Frankie was born.

We thought we were going for a trip to the seaside and were all screaming with excitement. Everybody was waving and cheering. We felt so lucky - two black taxis with all the children in them, and off we went.

At the time I wondered why my maw wasn't waving to us. I'm sure she was at the window crying. Then something was explained to Gussie, and she started crying and we followed suit. We didn't know why but were just told it would be okay. I have always remembered the Red Road being mentioned and then we arrived at this place called Smyllum Park.

Smyllum

When we arrived, we ran up the stairs to the front door of this lovely big house. The doorbell was rung, and a woman opened the it. As we stood there, I thought, she must be an angel with her large, white, flapping head dress and navy-blue clothes.

We were shown into a large room with huge, varnished furniture. Everything was spotless, holy pictures and statues. We were accompanied by Miss Hunter, the Welfare Officer in charge of us - she was very nice and dressed lovely. She spoke to the nun for a while then said cheerio and left.

Another nun came into the front room, which they called the parlour and, we were to learn later, was only used for special visitors. I don't recall ever being in that room again.

We were moved to a second room with the same kind of furniture. There we were given milk and biscuits and another nun came and took Gussie and Frankie away. Frankie was to be taken to the nursery, Louise and I were shown into what looked like a big, cobbled stone shed. It was very cold and dark, there was just one small wall lamp. An old man appeared with pillowcases of clothes for Louise and me. We were told to strip and to wait for him to give us our night clothes. I felt very uneasy, and it felt like forever that we had to stand there naked. Then Gussie came back, and she took Louise away to the nursery too. I was taken up to the dormitory.

The building was scary, with long dark, cold corridors that led into a place, like it was part of a house. This was where we were to live. We then went up a big, grand, highly polished, and varnished staircase which led into the dormitory. I was put into a bed in front of the nun's table. A light was on above my bed, and I couldn't sleep the whole night. I think I was there for a couple of nights and then I was moved further back into the dormitory. I was in what was known as 'The Lofties.'

A short time later, Louise was brought up to join me. She didn't settle in the nursery. I was so glad she was with me.

Late at night a buzzer would go off and everyone would shout out, 'Get the wet beds up,' then everyone would jump up and run to the toilet. Nobody spoke, it wasn't allowed. You couldn't sleep until that buzzer went. I had a bed wetter next to me, so I would help her. Most of the time it was too late, but as time went on, the nun in charge of us, Sister Appelene, would ask me to do little jobs. I felt at ease with her. She had a room at the end of the dormitory. I remember one girl, Lucy, cried all the time and Sister Appelene would tell me to take care of her. Louise and I would play with her and comfort her.

'She's the same as you, an orphan,' Sister would say.

I would tell Lucy, 'Me and Louise are going to be your big sisters,' which made her laugh.

One day the girl in the bed next to me had wet the bed and as there were some empty beds in our dorm, I changed sheets. I think that just happened twice because her sheet was dry, but her nightie was soaking, and the wee girl had to tell Sister that it was me that changed the sheet.

When the rest of us went for a wash and down for breakfast, the bed-wetter's were forced to sit in the wet bed with their sheets and nighties over their heads. We never ever found out what other punishment they had. So, Sister marched me down to the laundry because Gussie worked in there now. Gussie had to tell me off and made me promise not to do it again, which I never did.

Smyllum Routines

I was assigned to one of the smaller dormitories and given a bigger bed and put in charge. The food was disgusting, porridge every morning, mostly lumpy, and some days the milk was sour, but you had to eat it. Sister would stand over us to make sure we ate it up. Some of the children vomited it back up and we would be sent out. Again, we never knew what happened to them. Sunday breakfast was cornflakes, two slices of bread and a slice of bacon. I gave out the breakfasts and I got an extra slice of bacon and bacon fat to dip my second slice of bread in. We all loved the bacon fat. Some of the other kids would get extra fat and bread if they were good, but not the bed-wetters.

Dinners were big pots of cold mash potatoes with big hairy eyes still in them, all lumpy, with a block of margarine added for good measure. Puddings were mostly milk puddings, rice, custard, chocolate, sago, pink custard, usually sour or lumpy or both. If you could call it meat most of it was lumps of grizzle and because I collected the plates back in, anything Louise and I couldn't eat, I'd tell her to leave, and I would hide it in my knickers and get rid of it when I put the pots and plates to the lift outside. It was all disgusting.

We had some nice clothes with the school uniforms but old rags when we got home. Clean nightwear but in the winter, we wore thick nylon stockings and terrible knickers which were made of calico, a kind of rough denim. They fastened at the side with brass buttons and brass buttons front and back to hold our stockings up. God help you if you wet yourself wearing them. You'd end up all chaffed around your private parts and were made to stand in the corner with them on your head for hours at a time. Louise wet herself once. I had to rip a button off mine and kid-on I had to get another pair, which I did, and change hers as well as I oversaw the towels after bath for the laundry.

As for baths, one bath was run for about a dozen people. I think there was about three baths in total but don't know if they all got used.

The routine was rigid to say the least. In the mornings we would get up and have a quick wash with this horrible soap. It was cut off a big brown slab that smelled disgusting, worse than carbolic. It was very similar to the soap used for scrubbing the floors only the floor stuff was pink, but they both smelled the same. Then we would brush our teeth, without toothpaste. Brush our hair, everyone was given a large heavy wooden brush with metal prongs which scratched your head. Then we got dressed into uniforms went down and had breakfast and off to school. There we had school dinners, came back from school, and played for a little while. I don't remember what we got for tea, bread, and something I think, and then bed.

Weekends were the same in the morning, play for a while, if nice, play in the playground or go over to the fields which we all loved.

I remember my second day in Smyllum we were all sent over to the fields early morning. It was a lovely day, the dew was still on the grass, loads of rabbits running about and in the woods behind us. There was something wrong with their eyes. The big girl with us, our charge hand, said, 'You can't touch them as they have a disease called myxomatosis.'

Friday night was confessions at the Chapel. Saturday, sometimes you went into town to go to the pictures.

If it was wet or winter, we had to put on these big farmers' woollen socks, thick with polish on the soles. One child had a sack on the floor and the other would run around the floor pulling the child and sack it was great fun. The charge hand would splatter polish at different spots, and we had to polish the floor.

Sunday was Mass at the Chapel. we had lovely outfits for Chapel, black pleated skirts, little red jacket, and a black berry, so smart. The rest of the week after getting out of our lovely uniforms we were in old coats and clothes, pixie hats and knitted gloves with string going through our coats.

I think it was Sunday night we had our only bath of the week. Our hair would be treated for head lice which someone always had. I had to help bone comb some of the kids. Any lice found was put into newspaper. If I found nits or lice in their hair, Sister Appelene would then do their heads. It was really sore; they would get slapped if they cried.

Then Sunday tea was toad in the hole the only tea I remember us having. It was delicious, I can still remember the smell of it wafting all around. And then to bed.

We were allowed out to play in the playground on a Saturday if it was fine. It only had one roundabout. One day at the weekend was the only day we got to play with the babies. Gussie would hold two little sisters back for me and Louise to play with. One was Katie Boyle, which was the one I looked after, and Anne Boyle was the one Louise looked after. Gussie by this time was fifteen and had left school. She was asked to work in the nursery which she loved.

These two huge, corrugated steel doors would open for the children to join us in the playground. Everyone had their favourite. Everyone loved that time.

The Nursery

Katy, who I befriended, was about eighteen months old and Ann was about two and a half. Louise looked after Ann who couldn't talk properly. We later learned from Gussie it was because she had been burnt on her tongue. She also had a problem going to the toilet. A couple of times Gussie had to get the Sister in charge of the nursery, Sister Teresa, to help as part of her bowel would come down. After a couple of times of pushing it back up the Sister told Gussie not to bother her and she showed her what to do; how to push Anne's bowel back up. Gussie was left to do this.

Gussie and her friend Mary Connor, who worked with the little boys, including Frankie, had their own little staff room. Sometimes, when we were going to the toilet, I would knock the door and Gussie would give us biscuits and sweets. Once she told me when I came to her room, not to hang about because something awful had happened.

Gussie had found the baby she oversaw dead in his cot. He was poorly when he came into Smyllum earlier. Gussie, who oversaw bathing the children, had decided to bathe him first because of this and the fact that she only got one basin of hot water with which to bathe all the children with. Sadly, Gussie discovered him the next day. She ran to the Chapel to get the Sister. She was sent out and it was never mentioned ever again.

Gussie did see the parents one day and thought that they weren't very well looking. She never heard from the police or anyone to make a statement, nothing.

I remember several times being allowed to go over to the nursery to play with the children while Gussie had her tea. I can still see myself singing and highland dancing to the children.

Other Events

I had a lady who would write to me, just like a pen pal. Sister Appelene set that up for me. I can't recall much about what we wrote to each other, but I once said to her that I would love to have longer hair so I could put ribbons in. She sent me some beautiful ribbons. I was allowed to let my hair grow shoulder length; all the other children had to be to the ears.

Then I told her about Louise, she had already sent me a lovely cross and chain. Not long after, Louise and I received a beautiful thick gold bangle which was taken off us the next day. 'For safe keeping,' I was told. We never saw them again.

As for the gold chain I wore, I was sent over to the fields to play as I was off school for some reason. One of the big girls came over too, she had been allowed home for the weekend. When she saw my cross and chain, she asked me to take it off to look at it, which I did. She said she dropped the chain and even though we never moved I still couldn't find it.

I glared at her and said boldly, 'You've still got it!'

She replied, 'Shut up! No, I haven't.' Then she just cleared off.

I was really upset and had to tell Sister Appelene. She went to the Sister in charge of the big girls, Sister Louise, and whenever I passed her, she would shout at me in front of her girls, 'McKenna. This girl is a liar,' and she'd take my arms and hands and smacked them on the inside of my arms while holding my hands together.

I was moved downstairs to another dormitory. It was cosy, there were lovely shiny floor curtains and nice bedding. I remember being in that dorm a couple of times before when I wasn't well. I used to break out in cold sores around my mouth every winter. Sister Appelene would put wooden slats on the inside of my arms and bandaged them to stop me scratching. I would only be given toast and hot milk and an egg switched into it. The thought of it still makes me feel sick, even now.

If the Welfare Officer, Miss Waddell, came to see us, (which was only twice that I remember), that room was supposed to be our bedroom. However, it was all just for show - and with her about we were allowed to play with all the toys in the play hall. We were never allowed to do that at any other time, not even on Christmas Day.

At Christmas we all got a present, but they had to be put in the corner before going to bed and we were never allowed to play with them again.

I remember coming home from school one day and there was a lovely big metal horse, called Mobo. Mobo squeaked as it rocked, and it would squeak louder if ridden fiercely. We were allowed five minutes on it each, but it went with the rest of the toys.

One of the nuns, Sister Louise, from whom I suffered abuse over the years allowed me to grow my hair a bit longer which was considered a privilege. Sister Appelene oversaw us 'lofties' such as we were known and introduced me to a sort of pen pal which we called a new auntie. We would write to each other, and she would send me gifts. First, she sent me a gold chain and cross. I was allowed to wear it and keep it because it was considered Catholic. Then I got a gold bangle, and I told this auntie I had a sister called Louise and she got one too. We were only allowed to keep them just for the day. We got them and they were put away for 'safe keeping.'

Then I asked my new auntie if I had longer hair, I would love to have ribbons. She sent me a selection of them, and I was allowed to let my hair grow. One day I went to school with four long white satin ribbons that were kept in place with kirby grips. Lunch time came and we were running through Sister Louise's big hall to go to the toilet, my hair was all over the place and then we bumped into Sister Louise. Her eyes got bigger and rounder the moment she saw me. She opened her mouth and shouted 'McKenna, come here!'

I was terrified and whimpered, 'I have to go to the toilet.'

'Get to the toilet and then come back here.'

I hurried off. You didn't dare wet yourself as that would have made things worse.

She had a large pair of scissors with her, but her favourite punishment was to hold my hands together and slap the inside of my arms. On that occasion I remember crying, 'Mammy, Daddy,' as she did so.

'I'll give you mammy, daddy,' she said. 'You've not got any, that's why you're in here, nobody wanted you, you're an orphan,' then she took those scissors and cut my hair right up above my ears and sent me back to school. I was the laughing stock and to this day, 70 years on, I never got over it.

After the incident with my hair, Sister Appelene said she was going to 'Stop this once and for all.'

I don't know what happened but the next night I was moved into the big girl's dormitory which was run by Sister Louise. Everyone was ready for bed. I was told to first go to the toilet, then do my teeth, and get into my nightie. There was a girl at the basin, she was washing her knickers. I thought she had messed herself. I just went to the toilet, and then I heard someone shout at the girl, calling her a dirty little so and so, I heard her getting slapped with something, I was petrified. I came out of the toilet and saw the Sister hitting her and shouted, 'Sister!'

She stopped and shrieked at me to get out.

We were each given a big wooden hairbrush with metal prongs; that was what she was beating the girl with. The girl came running out after me thank goodness.

I jumped into bed. We weren't allowed to talk to each other. My bed was at the top of the dorm, and in front of one of the big girls in charge called Doreen. I heard Gussie's voice while I was in bed crying under the sheet, I was upset with what had happened to the other wee girl. I looked up and saw Gussie talking to Doreen, the charge of the big girls.

Gussie was dressed up in a beautiful navy velvet and taffeta evening dress and her friend Doreen was wearing a similar dress in green. I called to Gussie, she came over to me and asked why I was there. I didn't know. I told her I was terrified of Sister Louise as she was now called Mother Superior and that I had been sent to the dorm that very night.

'Just keep your head down and don't be cheeky to anyone,' she warned.

Gussie and Doreen were allowed out because they worked full time in Smyllum and they were friends, Gussie said she would try and find out what was going on.

A couple of days later it was summer camp time. All the big girls would go by coach to a summer camp for a fortnight. I was so glad that it was my time. We were all sitting around the big hall on benches. Sister Louise shouted out each girl's name. They were sent to a side room given the duffel bag with all their stuff and ushered onto the coach. Everybody was so excited. When it got to me being the remaining girl, she pointedly shouted to the driver, 'That's all.'

'Sister what about me?' I asked, feeling the tears rising at the back of my throat.

'No McKenna, you're being boarded out.'

I burst out crying, 'I need to tell my big sister Gussie.'

'She'll be told. Now go and get your sister Louise.' And with that she swept out of the room.

Miss Hunter, the welfare officer was waiting for us. She had Frankie with her, and we followed her out to the waiting taxi.

CHAPTER 2

Being fostered and onto Barrholm

We arrived at a house in Paisley to a foster family. They had a son, Patrick, who was around 13 years of age. I didn't like him from the start, and he didn't like us. He was a bully, especially to Frankie.

There was also an older brother who had a farmhouse in Linwood, he had just got married. His wife had a sister called Mary who had a calliper on her leg, and I think she had special needs. We went to stay with them one weekend and after tea he told Mary to wash up. He was constantly shouting at her. I watched him go into the kitchen and start shouting at her. I followed him and saw him slap her on the face.

I screamed, 'Leave her alone.'

This was all because she hadn't washed the dishes properly.

The next day when his mother came to collect us, she was told not to bring us back because I gave him a lot of cheek.

I did like staying in our foster home, we had lovely clothes, were allowed to go out and play and were taken out to meet other families - but I always felt I didn't belong. We were always being told we were orphans and fostered. Miss Powers was a bit strict, but her husband was lovely.

Then one day Miss Hunter, the welfare woman, came to take us on to somewhere else. She was saying it didn't work out. We were taken to the train station to a care home in Largs, Barrholm, but nothing was ever said to us why.

We arrived at Barrholm and the matron let us in. We went to a side room for a short while. Miss Hunter left, and the matron took us into the play hall and left us there to make our own friends.

The next day a doctor came to check that our health was okay. He checked our eyes, ears, and back. I had started having sore ears all the time. I put it down to Sister Louise smacking me around the ears or pulling me by them. It was always my fault according to her. She did it especially when I was going through the dark corridors on Fridays and Sundays going to Chapel. She would stand at the end of the corridor and when I got to her, she would grab me by the ears, smack me and say, 'I know it was you, McKenna, doing all the laughing and talking.' I never fully understood why I was always getting picked on by her.

It was okay at Barrholm, I did have some happy times, but matron wasn't very nice. She didn't really get involved with the children much, she didn't come to see us. All day-to-day stuff was left to the charges, I got on well with them all. We had a lot of freedom. I especially liked Mary Kirkwood. Sometimes I was invited to her boyfriend's family's house, as they were getting married. They surprised me one day by asking me to be a bridesmaid. I was over the moon.

Then there was the cook, I really got on well with her. I went for her Sunday papers and ginger. I was allowed to keep the money for the empty bottles and the shilling she gave me too. I also went to the butchers on a Saturday for her, butcher meat, vegetables, and bread. I would go to her house, her husband was so nice too, he had problems and couldn't hear. I would write things on a board that you could rub out, we had great conversations.

Bina was another charge hand I got on well with and even the cleaner Vi. To me she seemed as though she was in her forties, but she could have been older or younger. We would pop into her house in the town centre. We would go to the Mission Hall every weekend; she lived in a wee flat across the road from there. She told us that if ever we wanted to go up just to go ahead. She would let us dress up and put makeup on, it was great fun, and she was very kind.

I wasn't keen on school. Miss Gorman was my teacher; she wasn't very friendly. I remember two children; blonde twins were brought to our class. We were told they were Hungarian refugees. I think there was a war with Hungary and another country, but I didn't really understand about those things at the time.

Miss Gorman brought them to me and said 'You look after them. They're the same as you, orphans.'

Things like that were often said to me.

The twins' names were Gabriel and Gabriela. They were lovely and couldn't speak any English. It didn't matter though, we managed to communicate anyway.

I enjoyed teaching them but they were only with us for a couple of weeks. I went into school one day and they didn't appear. I was told they had been sent back - it really upset me.

Then I went to the seniors, an hour away on the bus. I met a girl who had been in Smyllum, but she didn't want to know as she was back with her parents, and I was in another home. She told her friend, 'Don't play with her, she's an orphan,' and then they sent me to Coventry leaving me left out.

I was allowed to befriend an old lady who was an invalid and housebound because she was in a wheelchair. She lived in a tenement building two up. I would visit her on Thursdays after school. I'd take her a bucket of coal and get her some sweets and juice from the shop. We would sit at the open window and anyone going by she knew something about them, she was a right wee gossip, but I loved it. Each week she gave me half a crown for keeping her company. I had to get permission from the home to visit her – the home would set up the visits. She would be sitting at the window watching me coming home from school. When she saw me, she would wave and then shout to say she would let me in. She was so happy, all full of smiles and gave me a hearty welcome.

Christmas time the home would take us to see a show, the first musical I ever saw was Oklahoma. I loved it. It was thrilling and from there I wanted to go on stage. To this day my favourite song is Oklahoma, and my favourite film is Tammy with Debbie Reynolds. Both had a lot of gingham material – I still love that material now.

When I moved into the senior school, one boy had just left that term. He was very handsome and popular, Tony Curtis hairstyle and good looking. He came down in the lunchtime to chat to everyone on his bike. At the time there was a craze for everyone jagging you with pins. The boy told everyone to leave me alone. From that day he came by to see me and he would ask me to go to the beach for a walk at lunch break. After a couple of weeks, he wanted to be my boyfriend. I loved him.

When we got on the bus to go home, he would always be at the gates and follow on his bike. This only went on a short while because I was only there temporarily.

.oOo.

Years later I used to go to the Bedford Bingo in Glasgow, and I met a couple of gay boys, and we were very good friends. I knew I knew him, and I said to him, 'Craig, where do you come from – not from here?'

He said, 'I'm not from here in Glasgow, I was born and bred in Ardrossan where I went to school,' he had the same jet black tony Curtis style hair, so handsome.

I asked, 'What's your dad's name?'

He said, 'Tommy.'

I said, 'Your dad was my first boyfriend, he used to come to my school.'

Craig said, 'Josie, my dad couldn't accept that I was gay. So, whenever I hear the song Tammy, it always reminds me of him.'

.oOo.

They also took us to an old people's home to entertain the old people there. It was always me that got picked to give them a song. I only knew two songs. Also, because I'd learned Highland dancing when I was in Smyllum I was asked to dance. The old folk would give us threepence or a penny for entertaining them. After such experiences I'd always dreamed of taking to the stage or going to drama school but didn't know how to go about it.

When I was at school my teacher would do a drama hour. She would ask volunteers to come up to do a scene, but the other kids would tell me that I couldn't do it because I was an orphan, otherwise I would have been right up there. Opportunities were lost on me because lack of money and connection – nobody encouraged me with anything.

Miss Cousin, another charge, was very nice. She used to tell stories; she made them up as she went on. I thought that was great.

Then one day ma maw appeared. She had only visited us twice while were in Smyllum and after that we were told she was dead. I recall the playroom door opening and matron coming in with a woman in a long fur coat, hat, bag and gloves. Matron shouted, 'McKenna family!'

So I took Frankie and Louise over to her.

'This is your mother,' said Matron.

I thought she was a film star. I was told to shake her hand. I curtsied and told Frankie and Louise to do the same. I really thought she was another foster mother.

We sat for about half an hour and then she left. She told us she was re-marrying and coming back and see us with her new husband which she did. One day about six months later I came home from school, and we were told we were leaving and going to live in England with our new family.

CHAPTER 3

Moving to England – the early days

I was fourteen and a half by the time we moved to England. My friend had left school and stayed on at the home as a carer and that's what I wanted to do but was told I had to leave. I was unhappy about it. A couple of days later we left, made our way to Glasgow Central, where we were met by Gussie.

We stayed at a house of another sister called Bridie, who we didn't know. I didn't like the house. It only had a room and outside toilet. We all had to sleep in one bed as she had a wee girl aged five. Her husband had to sleep in a chair.

We left the next day and Gussie took us to Central Train Station again and we got a train to Corby where we were met by our brother Eric who we hadn't seen for years since we left Smyllum. I had forgotten all about him.

He introduced himself 'I'm your brother Eric.'

I didn't recognise him. He completely understood the reasons why.

We arrived at the house, 25 Blake Road, Corby. It was a brand-new big house. Spotless inside, nice furniture, not much but enough. Ma maw's new husband had three sons who were living there too. I also met three more brothers I didn't know I had.

Later, the sister from Glasgow appeared shortly after with her husband and daughter May. I didn't like that sister Bridie from day one.

When we arrived at Corby some of our beautiful clothes and things went missing. She had taken them and now they were living with us too. Her husband got a job, I liked her husband James, he was a hard worker.

So now it was very overcrowded in the house. It never stopped, other members of the family would come and stay with their families. We were always struggling. Our electricity and gas were often cut off. We had to light candles at night, and food was cooked on the fire. Different families coming and going all the time and ma maw always ill or in hospital. I had started to bond with ma maw. I would tell her to get rid of Bridie and that I would look after her.

I don't know how, but Eric and Tom and one of my stepfather's sons joined the army - some of the others left. I did notice ma maw didn't or couldn't handle Frankie. I was sure she didn't like him, always telling me to take him away from her, never speaking to him and saying that I had to deal with him, and he always felt that way too.

The eldest brother James

As he got older, it got worse, another brother James appeared, the eldest of the boys. He had brought a girlfriend; he wasn't very nice. Ma maw was terrified of him, the other brothers too. He was continually bullying and hitting them. He was always out drinking and coming back drunk, at the time his girlfriend was pregnant. I felt sorry for her.

One night he had gone to bed drunk. I went up to the bathroom to get ready to go out to meet my boyfriend Fraser. James shouted on me from his bedroom, 'Josie, come here.' When I went in to see what he wanted he told me to sit on the bed and asked me about Fraser. Then he suddenly grabbed me, threw me down next to him and tried to kiss me, forcing his tongue down my throat. I fought him off and ran down the stairs with the sound of him roaring with laughter in my ears. I ran along to Fraser's house, so upset. I told his mother and him what had just happened and then later, after I had calmed down, he took me back home.

Fraser finished with me at the time because his mother said, 'Stay away from that family if that's what they're like.'

We did get back together eventually, but when I went back to Scotland, that put paid to us.

.oOo.

Years later I was in Kettering, married with children and working in the Bingo near to my house. I used to make the teas and sandwiches, his sister came up. She couldn't believe it, after all these years and said, 'Wait till I tell Frazer, he's here too.'

He came to see me a couple of days later and asked to go back out with him.

I told him, 'Oh, no, I'm married with four children.'

Years later I heard that he died very young at the age of 36. I found out on New Year's Eve. It was sad at the time because he was really my first love.

.oOo.

I never would be in James's company again. I hated him but was scared to tell anybody else except Louise. We just stayed out of his way. A short time later, he left with his girlfriend because the Police were looking for him. I think ma maw phoned them; all I said to ma maw was get rid of him please.

He did come back again for a short while, his girlfriend had had the baby, but they weren't able to settle and had to leave because the police and other people were looking for him.

CHAPTER 4

Back to Scotland

Another sister, May, and kids came to stay for a while but after a couple of weeks it fell on me to take them back to Scotland. I didn't know what her situation was, but I was instructed to take her to another sister, Ella's house. She was told she couldn't stay there and that I was to help her round to her ex-husband's which I did.

When we got there an old man answered the door. I was left to look after the kids while they discussed their business. They went into another room and when they came out told me to return to Ella's house.

'Is that your husband?' I asked May,

'Yes,' she said 'We were married when I was sixteen. It was arranged by our maw because apparently, he had money. At the time he was known as the moneylender, buying and selling goods.'

This moneylender man turned out to be my sister Ella's husband's father. It took years for me to find out the whole story about that. Nobody ever spoke about anything, you only found out things by mistake. I once had to ask May what my father was like.

She replied, 'If you see Eric, that's what your father's like.'

So, I had to stay with Ella, her husband John and their three kids. I started school in St James, Paisley. Ella was a bit strict, but John was nice. I had to look after the kids a lot. I'll admit, was a bit frightened of Ella, she was always arguing and shouting at John.

During that time my hair was really long. I loved my hair. One Sunday evening, Ella sent me out to get the kids in for a bath for school next day. I knew where they would be, playing in a friend's back door. There was a boy I fancied at the time, he was there with a group of other teenage boys, and we were all playing. I forgot the time.

The boy I fancied said, 'Josie, do you want a drag on of my fag?'

I didn't smoke but to act big I took it. Just as he was handing it to me my sister Ella came around the corner and spotting me she started shouting terrible names. She chased me all round the streets and when she got me home gave me a terrible hiding.

Every Saturday night Ella would go round to her friend, Isabel's house with a couple of neighbours. They would have a wee drink and sing along. Ella hadn't spoken to me all week and on the Saturday teatime she said, 'You're not babysitting tonight; you're coming round to Isabel's house. Wash your hair and get ready.'

I thought she had forgiven me.

We went round a bit early, there was another woman there, I made them all tea. I felt really happy listening to them telling wee stories, having a great laugh, and looking forward to the sing song.

Ma maw's favourite song was '*Forever and ever*,' and '*It was only a bunch of violets*,' African violets were her favourite flowers. I sang those songs but after a while the other lady rubbed her hands together and said, 'So let's get started.' and she placed a chair in the middle of them and commanded, 'Josie sit there.'

The lady pointedly addressing Ella said, 'How short do you want it?'

I was told that the lady was a hairdresser, so I thought I was to have a hairdo.

'Right up above the ears,' said Ella, she didn't even look at me.

'No I don't want my haircut,' I cried, pleading.

'Shut up,' said Ella. 'If you want to act like a prostitute you'll be treated like one.'

I didn't even know what she meant.

The woman cut my hair really short despite my protestations. I cried quietly throughout the whole process. Afterwards I was sent back to the house. I was in a dreadful state but managed to find a pen and paper and wrote to ma maw about what Ella had done and said I wanted to come back home.

CHAPTER 5

Corby

Ma maw and brother George got someone to drive them up to Paisley to fetch me back. There was an almighty row between ma maw and Ella and then we left.

We didn't last long in Corby but some of my happiest early memories are rooted there.

After coming out of care was when we went to live in Corby. It was just a new town moving into a lovely big brand-new house. Everything was new and fresh and a to me it represented brand new life to go with it, or so I thought. Rock and roll was the music era which I loved; it was the late fifties and early sixties. My favourite singers at the time were Perry Como, Dean Martin, Connie Francis, Alma Cogan. The sixties was Cliff Richards, Billy Fury, The Shadows, Buddie Holly, Brenda Lee and of course, later, Simon and Garfunkel, also country and western, sorry no Elvis, The Beatles or Rolling Stones or the likes.

My favourite song on the karaoke or sing song is still Cliff's Travelling Light. I can't see the words properly on the screen, so they let me sing it by myself (a Capello). The era also ended up with Ali's favourite, 'This is dedicated to the ones I love,' by the Mamas and Pappas.

From Corby we moved again, right back to Scotland, then back to England. We moved all the time. And just like ma maw, we brought with us the laundry basket that she used for every flitting to carry her white linens in. It was part and parcel of the landscape of our lives.

Kettering

We moved to a house in Kettering, near Corby, 25 Albert Street but like before, this became overcrowded. Bridie and her family moved in again.

I started working a shoe factory called Dolcis. I worked as a stamper. This entailed using a little slab where I had to make up the numbers, the stamp was red hot for stamping in the shoe sizes and numbers. I stamped my arm more than I did the shoes. At the time I had a boyfriend called Roy. Frankie was getting into all sorts of trouble, staying out late, never being about the house. That brother James was in prison in Bedford and wrote to ma maw saying he was getting out. Everybody was dreading it. I didn't know the full extent of him or what he was capable of, I just hated him. When he got out, he came to us but didn't stay long and went back to Scotland.

My brother George was great, he took charge of everything. He was the one that got rid of James.

Myself, Louise, and Bridie's daughter May, slept upstairs in one room in a double bed. It was sectioned off in the middle by a curtain. At the bottom of our bed was another single bed where our brother Rab slept and at the other end of the room was another double bed for my 2 stepbrothers. They were okay, I ended up good friends with one of them, Billy. Allan the other one, was shy and quiet and didn't mix with anyone. We were all working except Louise and Frankie and Bridie was having another baby.

First meeting with Roy

My husband Roy told me once what it was that first attracted him to me was my lovely long dark hair and I had a fine pair of child-bearing hips. I think that was a compliment, he wasn't wrong about that. Gussie had a near miss there, because Roy had asked Gussie out on a date first, but she knocked him back. My brother George told Roy him about his other sister Josie who was coming back from Paisley, and he would introduce him to me. (None of Gussie's or my kids knew about that story till recently, they were shocked. Which is amusing.)

The story of how I got to go out with Roy is an odd one. I fancied a boy called Terry, who had a mate called Roy. I had a date with Terry one Saturday night and he didn't appear but sent Roy to apologise. Roy then asked me if I would like to come out with him. I wasn't old enough to go to the pub, so we just went round to the Club. And by and by we became a couple.

Sometimes I would go round to meet Roy at the pub. I would stand outside of the window, and he would pass me out

29

a juice. When he left the pub, we would go for a walk and then home again.

Once again things weren't good in the house, ma maw was always going up to Scotland for some reason, but we were never told why. The electric and gas was always getting cut off. Sometimes George got someone to connect it back on or because it was on a coin metre everybody had a key to open the metre which you passed on to people for a small charge. The key was filed down to fit the meter. I remember being told don't leave your wardrobe key in the wardrobe as it would be stolen for precisely that reason. Another way of working the meter was by filing a ½ penny down the one side so it would fit like a shilling for the metre.

When I lived with Ella whenever her gas was cut off she'd get someone to reconnect it using a bicycle tube to connect the pipe to another.

One day when the house was freezing, and Ella had gone to the shops, I put all the gas rings on, opened the oven and put my feet in it. It was great, my toes were toasty. I didn't realise Ella had left the front door open. (I had always been warned not to answer the door, especially to the gas or electric men.) The gas man walked straight in and into the kitchen.

His jaw fell open when he saw me with my feet in the oven, the bicycle tube connection and all the gases blazing. Fortunately, Ella appeared and sent the gas man packing. She told him to knock the door when she was in - which he did - but she wouldn't answer.

I remember hearing him shout, 'I'll get the police,' that worried me a bit. He hung about for a while but eventually left.

At which point I was sent round to get the man to disconnect the pipes properly.

I don't know what happened after that and didn't realise at the time just how dangerous it was. Everyone was in the same situation and helped each other out. But not everything was good.

CHAPTER 6

My late teens

I had started going out with Roy by this time and as I said things started happening to me by an older brother – his name, I still hate saying, was Rab. He was a heavy drinker but was always working. He brought a wage into the house. If you didn't bring money into the house, you couldn't stay.

At times Rab would come in drunk and we dreaded him coming up to the room because he had started to try to interfere with me. I didn't know until a few years later that Louise and May heard him next to me crouching down on the floor with his hands all over me under the bedclothes. They would kick me to wake me, I would wake suddenly and shout at them before realising what was happening.

After that, I'd waken to the sound of him peeing in the corner of the room. I'd run downstairs and stay there until he had fallen asleep, too scared to tell ma maw or Bridie. I was sure we would have been blamed, so I told my brother George who was the only person I trusted, he was always sorting things out.

Once I had bad period pains and had to lie down. Ma maw gave me a couple of aspirins and told me to go to bed. I had fallen asleep when Rab had come home drunk, I woke with him attempting to interfere with me again.

It was after this incident I told George. I think he must have told ma maw because the next day I was told to move into ma maw's room downstairs. When I moved to her room, she said to me, 'You'll be alright now, he's out the house.'

It was a relief, but nothing was ever said about it, and he was put out the house.

My room was to the front, you didn't hear much from the sitting room and kitchen which were to the back of the house. One day my window was rattled and then the front door was knocked. I thought it was someone I knew so went to open the front door.

Rab stood there with another guy, Tony, and I just froze.

He said his friend Tony had a job for me – to make some money. He claimed Tony wanted to take some photos of me, 'Just topless,' he said it like it was no big deal.

I screamed for George, and they ran off. George and I were the only ones in the house at the time. George came running out and went after them, but they disappeared. We didn't see them again for some time.

George moved to Scotland and eventually married and with him gone we moved again to another house in Kettering, King Street.

It was around that time I started suffering from a scalp condition. My scalp became so badly scabbed I had to have my head shaved. It may have become that way because of the hairspray that everyone used at the time. The hairspray was called Bellaire and was like glue. What with that and the stress I was going through with what was going on with me, ma maw bought me a wig. Unfortunately, the shop only had a grey one, so I dyed it black which made it feel like straw. I would put my rollers in and just wear a headscarf. Everybody would do that for days at a time.

We moved to Glasgow again for a short time, Argyle Street. I was always telling the kids stories, especially the Hoolit. Ma maw and Bridie would tell me to amuse the kids and tell them a story. I would always say to myself, *kids love scary stories*. So, a scary story they would have, they would start to scream, eyes wide with fear, but tell me to keep telling them more. I made up the stories as I went along, even the grown-ups laughed. Just watching their faces was so funny.

The Hoolit was a made-up monster dog or sheep. I'd get to a part where I was outside the door and someone was pulling me back by the hair and because I had my wig on, I'd use my hand to pull me back and of course, the wig would come off. I wish we had videos of back then. It was a classic, all their faces and screams. Gussie, Bridie, and my maw wetting themselves with laughter and then I'd put the wig back on. I'd get some strange looks; they couldn't work it out.

While staying there Roy sent me his wages every week – of course it went to ma maw. Sometimes he would send me a present, a gold locket always accompanied with poetry he had written. If I started to read my letters and the poem ma maw would shout, 'Never mind that rubbish, how much did Roy send you?' That was maw.

Then we went back to King Street in Kettering. After being there a while, Rab was allowed back to the house because he was working, although was not allowed in if he had been drinking. I just kept out of his way. I didn't see much of him at all. Then my other sister May arrived with her kids. She had separated from her husband and ma maw let her stay for a short time – then things started happening to May with that brother.

A mattress was put in the back sitting room on the floor for May. There was no room upstairs. We were overcrowded again. May told me one night that he was pestering her and not to leave her with him. He would just sit in the corner not saying a word, waiting till everyone went to their beds. I'd stay put until eventually he went up. Once I heard him creeping downstairs again, trying to get to May's bed.

'Leave her alone,' I shouted then screamed for ma maw. When she came down, I told her he was pestering May and had tried it with me too. I begged her to get the police, but she just threw him out the house claiming, 'We don't bring the police to our door – forget about it and it won't happen again.'

From the stories she told me May had a hard life. I liked her, she was the only one to come to see us when we were in Barrholm. I didn't really know her, but she told me she was our sister. I remember when she came to stay with us at Albert Street in Kettering. I had just started going out with Roy. May was with us for about two weeks, that was about long enough for maw, especially with three young kids. I was told to help May and the kids move back to Scotland. While I was getting things together Roy appeared, and maw shouted at him to go into the back kitchen. Then they both came into the front room, which was my room and maw said, 'Roy's coming to Scotland with you. He has my permission.'

CHAPTER 7

Scotland with Roy

I was sixteen and quite happy with the idea of Roy coming to Scotland with us. He went to his digs to collect his things while I sat outside waiting for him. When he came out his jacket pockets were bulging with something and when I asked him what it was, he said, 'Tins of salmon and I'm going to give some to your mother,'

When we got home, he went straight into the back kitchen, we left shortly after, taking the bus back to Glasgow.

As we were travelling back Roy repeated the conversation, he had had with ma maw. He said he had asked her permission to marry me, and she agreed. Strangely he still had two tins of salmon. I asked him where's the other four? He said he had given them to ma maw. She had then advised him to give her his digs money on the understanding that when we returned from Glasgow, he would stay with us. It probably amounted to £10 or £20. Either way, I wasn't happy because to me it seemed like I had been sold for four tins of salmon plus the dig's money.

When we arrived at Paisley, we went straight to my sister Ella's house. May and her kids went off to somewhere else. Roy and I stayed with Ella and John for a few weeks and then I started feeling unwell so went to the doctors where he informed me that I was pregnant. I couldn't quite take it in. When I told Ella she wasn't very happy.

'Go back to Kettering, right now. I'm not getting the blame for this,' she said, Ella just didn't want the responsibility and made us leave there and then.

We had no money, there were no phones, and it would have taken too long for a letter to arrive at maws with the news. So, out of desperation, we went to a police station in Glasgow and stayed there overnight. They kept us in the cells with the gate open. I was then taken to a children's home for a night where they got us on the train to Kettering and informed maw – they didn't believe I was sixteen as I was very small for my age.

CHAPTER 8

Expecting

When we arrived at ma maw's I told Roy we were finished as I was scared to tell maw I was pregnant. So, Roy had to go back to his parents and for the next six months I didn't see or have any contact with him.

I was eight months pregnant before anyone knew about my condition. Fortunately, I managed to get my old job back at Dolcis Shoe factory which made things seem normal, but I was beginning to feel quite unwell. Rather than ask anyone in my family I asked a woman at work to come to the doctors with me. I told her I had kidney stones and needed an adult to accompany me. At the time I did suffer from kidney stones and wasn't sure if that was the reason why I wasn't feeling well.

When I saw the doctor, he confirmed that I was pregnant and had a kidney infection. So, I left my job in the shoe factory, I was embarrassed in case anyone noticed my condition. There was a lot of shame attached to being an unmarried mother in those days. From there I went to work in a laundry, but the work was telling on me, I was feeling faint nearly every day.

I had confided in my stepbrother Billy about my condition and one day, while coming home for lunch I had had enough. My ankles were swollen, and I couldn't hide it any longer. I was nearly eight and a half months pregnant by then. One day Billy was just coming out of the house when he happened to mention that Bridie also knew.

The midwife had come round to visit Bridie as she had recently had a baby. She had spotted my condition and asked Bridie what she was doing about Josie and her pregnancy, she hasn't been to see us for a while. It was a shock to Bridie as she didn't know what she was talking about.

'Josie isn't having a baby,' she claimed. 'It's the big stick out underskirts she wears.' The midwife smiled and said, 'I know the difference between a stick out skirt and a pregnant girl.'

So, after she had gone and everyone had returned to work, Bridie made a cup of tea and a sandwich. At the time I had my feet in a basin of water, I didn't want to go back to work.

Bridie just came out with it. 'Right, how far along are you?'

I burst into tears and said I was eight and a half months gone. She was shocked as she thought I was only a couple of months along. She told me she was going to send a telegram to our mother as she was in Scotland, staying with May at the time.

May had been in hospital after being assaulted. She had to earn money in other ways which she didn't like to do. It was hard on her health, but she did it as a means of supporting her kids.

She had become an alcoholic too. I hadn't seen much of her for years. Her children had grown up and May had then met someone who was very good to her and supported her. I never met him, but she idolised him. She had given up drinking and he helped her with her AA meetings. Sadly, he died and when he did, despite being devastated she managed to stay off the drink and took charge of her granddaughter from a very early age as her mother, May's daughter, was having problems with drink.

Unfortunately, when May's granddaughter was about sixteen, May's health deteriorated, and she passed away.

That was over twenty years ago now. Her granddaughter now has three children of her own. I know May would have been proud of them and spoiled each of them rotten.

.oOo.

Louise was fifteen when she left school. She was staying at King Street in Kettering at the time. The day before her fifteenth birthday she went to Dolcis Shoe Factory to apply for a job. She was told to come back when she was fifteen. So, she went back the next day. The surprised receptionist said, 'Louise, you have to be fifteen to start work.'

Louise said, 'I am, it's my fifteenth birthday today.'

The receptionist was so impressed with Louise she informed the manager who promptly gave her a job. She was in the shoe factory industry for fifty-three years and ended up with that, manager's job. Ironically, she got the position from the same manager who gave her the job in the first place.

Louise left our King Street home after she started work. She hated staying in our house, mostly because of what had happened to me and because there was never enough to eat or clothes to wear. The constant moving from place to place plus the gas, or the electric being cut off and having to use candles was terrible and enough to make her decide to leave.

Louise moved in with a lovely couple who really looked after her, showed her how to open a bank account and how to work her money and savings. Then she met her future husband Trevor and eventually they went on to get married. They were a perfect couple. Trevor was a hard worker and a great provider. They bought their first house, a lovely bungalow. I was so proud of Louise for what she achieved in such a short time after leaving our house. Unfortunately, she was slagged constantly for getting on. This was probably because she didn't give anything towards our house.

I wasn't bringing in much money because I had my daughter Bev. Ma maw said I had to find somewhere else to live as she wanted to take in some paying workers. I ended up staying with a woman who had four kids. The house was overrun with mice. When I went to bed and pulled the bed clothes back it was full of mice, they would scurry onto the floor. I had to leave the lights on all night. I was only there for a few weeks – looking after her kids in exchange for free digs while she went out to work. Unbeknownst to me she had been working as a prostitute. I had already told Louise I didn't like staying there and she said she would ask our maw if I could go back home.

The next day the police came to the house because the woman didn't come home all night – she had been arrested. There was a couple of other people with the police who were social workers. They had come to take the children into care.

Louise came to tell me to come back home, I was so relieved to leave. Things had improved a bit more by then. I started work again, back at Dolcis. Bridie and maw looked after Bev; she was nearly two.

Strangely maw would call to Bev. 'Sylvia, come over here.'

This happened a few times until I said 'Maw, why do you keep calling Bev, Sylvia? Who is Sylvia?'

She replied quietly 'it's a long story. I'll tell you about it one day.' But she never did.

Bridie was standing in the kitchen and heard her and gave out a funny look. I didn't really pay it much attention.

She was always in and out of hospital because she had developed tuberculosis (TB)

Both George and her husband had to go into Rushden Sanitorium for a time because of the TB.

Bridie was left in charge of the house. I visited everyone in the Sanitorium a couple of times a week. It was quite a distance and awkward getting there. Ma Maw also had diabetes, she and her husband came out of hospital, but George had to stay in to have an operation to remove one of his lungs. He stayed in much longer and I was tasked with bringing his girlfriends to visit him. I would have to give them time alone and so would go out into the gardens to pass the time with other patients. I enjoyed those times and George always knew where to find me.

Ma maw was always in hospital in Kettering on account of her diabetes, it had been bothering her quite a lot – then, once again, she moved back to Glasgow. I was married with my own house when she was taken into Mearns Kirk hospital where she passed away – it was 1969.

CHAPTER 9

Argyle Street then Paisley 1963

After leaving Argyle Street in Glasgow, we moved to Well Street in Paisley. My mother, stepfather Willie Spiers and myself moved there. I was pregnant with my second child Tina. The move meant I had to change doctors, and when I went into labour, I was sent to Lennox Castle in Lennox town, Stirlingshire - as there were no beds available nearer.

Roy was back in Kettering working and had put his name down for a house there. I was in hospital for over two weeks and when Tina was born, she had black hair and was very dark skin. George and I were the same at birth.

I think George was living in Glasgow at this time and had got married. Roy had come to Paisley when I had Tina but didn't get to visit me once. I later learned he stayed with my mother and had a suitcase filled with new suit and other clothes and of course, some holiday pay. The whole suitcase contents were intended for the pawn shop. Bridie took the clothes there to get money on loan. As a result, he had to wear pyjamas all week and couldn't visit me all the time he was there.

Instead, George visited every day making excuses that Roy wasn't well. He suffered from asthma and a skin condition, eczema. I wasn't happy but knew he couldn't help it. Of course, it wasn't true, girls in the next beds would say 'Oh, you can tell who the father is there.' I had to tell them George was my brother.

Lennox Castle was a bit out of the way and took a while to get to it. Apparently, years before it had been an asylum for girls who had been getting into trouble, or their parents couldn't control them or wayward girls who fell pregnant at a young age.

It had a section for special needs teenagers who could work and at 7.30 am we were wakened by them going to work singing the song from the film Snow White and the Seven Dwarfs, 'Hi Ho, Hi Ho, it's off to work we go.' We would all look out the window watching them. They were all so happy with their shovels, God love them, it was a picture.

When I was due to leave George came to get me. Roy had gone back to Kettering, but he always sent me a letter and left me some money and told me my mother had money that he had lent her. Roy didn't know my mother very well and I knew I wouldn't see any of it again.

We left the hospital, me Tina and George and walked to the bus stop. We had to go to Glasgow first. When I realised, we weren't going back to Paisley, George explained once again, we were going to another house in Kinning Park, McLelland Street.

Gussie was in one close, Bridie in another, my mother in one and my brother John in another. John didn't stay long so my mother put me into his house, and he moved round the corner to Howwood Street. We were moved again, one at a time. I just thought this is what happens, nobody every explained why. It was only years later that I was told the true and real reason why.

Gussie always paid her own way; she had had a baby that she named Alan after her husband. He worked away and often visited and took care of her. At the time we were all staying in a room and kitchen each in Howwood Street.

There was a money lender in the area, it wasn't long before my mother and Bridie got to know him and began borrowing from him. They must have thought they had won the pools. The system was that once someone had become established with the lender and taken out a loan they were seen as the point of contact for any other loans. Generally, a name was given, and a sum of money lent to that name. However, there was no system for knowing whose name had or hadn't been added within the family, it was easily abused by less than scrupulous people. Bridie set this up at first. Initially she used my mother's name to get a loan and then she used her own name to get another loan. Gussie, John, and I never knowingly took a loan but had heard of Beef Leslie the money lender. Gussie wouldn't allow her name to be used but Bridie used our names without our consent – we never saw the money and were just told 'that's what was happening.'

One day, Beef Leslie turned up at the door looking for money that had been lent to someone called Roy. It was Roy who answered the door and told Beef Leslie he didn't know anything about owing any money. Bridie was supposed to pay for the loan she had taken out in Roy's name and didn't, so I had to borrow more money to pay Beef Leslie. Fortunately, I kept friends with Beef Leslie's elderly mum and ended up

45

having to and speak to her and ask her to ask him to come and see me.

Beef Leslie would stand at the end of the road every morning at a certain time waiting for people to come and pay him his money or borrow something.

I couldn't wait to get away from the area and everyone associated with it. Gussie and Alan moved to Corby into a new house. They were glad to get away too.

By then I was pregnant again with my daughter Alison. She was born in that house; my friend next door was called Rae Alison (Sarah). Roy and I both loved the name Alison as a first name after Rae. She was a good friend. She was separated from her husband and had two children. Caroline was three years old, and she was pregnant with her little boy Billy. I helped the midwife deliver Billy. It's the only time I've witnessed a birth and it was amazing. I later found out that we were indirectly related as Rae was Alan's niece. Then Rae met someone else and moved away. We promised to keep in touch.

I used to have credit in the corner shop, Bev would take Tina and other friends into the shop, and I would give her a note and put at the bottom, sweets for the kids. It ended up with about half a dozen kids getting sweets – she was taking too long one day so I went over to the shop and there was Bev sitting on top of the wee bags of coal, hands full of sweets surrounded by all her friends. I soon put a stop to that.

We lived in a wee side street, there were no cars or any transport – kids could play safely. Then, things changed when Roy managed to get us a house in Kettering at Linden Avenue.

I made arrangements to move and was so glad to have moved away.

CHAPTER 10

Howwood Street and onwards

While living in Howwood Street I fell pregnant with my third daughter Alison. At the time you got an extra payment of £28 for delivering the child at home. £28 was a lot of money back then and money was tight.

Everyone kept saying to me 'are you no bye yet or telling me to take a mix of castor oil and orange juice to bring my labour pain on. It did work eventually.

We had an outside toilet at the time, and it seemed like I spent 5 hours on that pan before my labour started. The whole street was told, and everybody made their way to my close, all lined up outside. My friend Ray, from next door, helped the midwife deliver Alison but shouted out to everyone 'it's a boy!' then had to shout out to everyone 'it's a girl.' Everyone thought I'd had twins. Ray had just got it wrong because the cord was caught between Alison's legs, giving her the wrong impression. It was an easy birth; everything went well and soon I was up and about again. Alison was three months old when we moved again, this time to Kettering.

After moving from Howwood Street, my mother got a house in Castlemilk, Glasgow. It was a brand-new high rise flat fourteen stories up, it was lovely. Every Saturday Maw and Bridie would disappear all day and say it was for the Barrows, where you bought everything very cheap. Curtains, bedding, lino and second-hand items and stalls. I later went there myself; it was a great day out I loved listening to the patter, cafes, especially the seafood café.

One time, Gussies sister-in-law came over to visit from Canada and bought Maw a lovely pair of net curtains with hand painted lilies on them. Maw was hanging them on the veranda window when Bev picked one of them up, ran out onto the veranda and chucked it over the railings. When we realised what had happened, I had to run down to look for it, but it was nowhere to be seen. Of course, Bev thought it was funny, Maw didn't.

Maw had a tick man that used to come regularly. I was allowed to get some things for the kids and pay for it weekly. I bought Bev and Tina lovely red woollen coats with black velvet collars and hats to match. They were really in fashion that year and were known as the prince Charles style for boys or girls and were finished off with black patent sandals. I said I would keep them new for travelling to Kettering when the time came but Maw and Bridie had other ideas and pawned the clothes along with my wedding ring.

Roy had got the keys for our house in Linden Avenue (Kettering) that week. Maw and Bridie had cleared off that day. I waited for them to return with my ring and the clothes from the pawn, but they didn't come back in time for me to catch my train. I was so upset and dreaded telling Roy about my ring I wrote a letter to Maw pleading with her to get my ring back along with Roy's clothes which she had also pawned. She did get them back to me eventually. I was back working in Dolci's shoe factory at the time. We never got the kids' clothes back though, even though Roy had sent the money on to her to get them back.

I always felt sorry for Maw, every sob story she fed me I believed; always about how unwell she was with nobody to turn to and asking if we would help her out.

Roy was very fond of my mother but didn't know the full extent of her and Bridies wheeling and dealing escapades.

Maw visited us once and stayed a couple of days. I don't know why she visited, she never ever said much. I think there was something else involved but I never found out what.

She went back to Scotland and I never saw her again as she died in 1969, I was at work in Dolci's when I got the message. Gussie and Louise were working there as well, they were great workers. I hated it but it was great money. Mrs Mason the personnel officer called us all together to break the news. She gave us time off to travel to Scotland for the funeral. We all felt a bit numb and a bit strange, none of us could cry. Frankie was told but didn't want to know.

We came back to Kettering the day after the funeral, and I don't think it was ever discussed again. As time went on though I started having feelings about missing my mother, especially when I told the kids stories my mother had told me. Bridie would always say, 'What are you two whispering about?'

And I'd say, 'Don't tell her.'

I think deep down Bridie didn't really like me, but the feeling was mutual.

The kids called my mother 'Granny Maw' and stepfather (Willie Spiers) 'Lollipop' because I called him Pop. That time when Maw visited it was near Christmas because I remember she brought presents. Bev got a nurse's outfit. Tina and Alison got cardboard handbags full of Edinburgh rock, they loved that and never forgot them so every time I went to Scotland, I bought them some. Even now they'll say, remember Granny Maw with the Edinburgh rock.

I found myself pregnant with my first son Brendon. He was born in Kettering at St Mary's maternity. Roy and I couldn't agree on a name, he wanted to name him Brendon after his brother and I wanted Simon after Paul Simon, from Simon and Garfunkel – I loved them, Roy liked them too. So, when I delivered the baby, the midwife asked the name I said I hadn't made my mind up yet and told her about Roy's choice.

'I got engaged last night,' said the midwife. 'Why don't you call him after my fiancé's name, Godfrey?'

I burst out laughing. I thought she was cracking a joke and said yes. So, the baby was called Godfrey for the first two weeks as she had stuck a label to his cot. I couldn't wait to see Roy's reaction to the name. He wasn't amused and tried to take the label off. I told him to leave it for now as the nurses have to call him something, which wasn't true. When Roy left, he went straight to the registry office and registered him, Brendon. I didn't tell anyone that story for years. Roy was too embarrassed and later, when Bren grew up, I knew he would be the same.

It was only after I had started to write my life story and was spending some time in hospital that Bev and Tina came to visit me. They asked if they could read my book, I said, 'Yes, it's for you all anyway,'

They read the bit about the boy's name and asked 'Mam, did you have another baby boy because who is this Godfrey?' I just laughed and explained the story.

Roy and my kids all have a great sense of humour, we see the funny sides of everything.

Back in Kettering, three years after giving birth to Brendon, I found myself pregnant again. I had another son, Simon. After Bren's birth the doctors said they were quite concerned about the weight of my babies as they got smaller with each pregnancy. Bev was 8 1/2 lbs, Tina was 7 ½ lbs, Alison 6 ½ lbs, Bren 5 ½ lbs. They also told me to give up smoking, which I did, I was in pretty good health and always went back to my original weight, which was 8 stone, very quickly. With Simon it was a different story. I went up to 13 ½ stone. I worried more about losing the baby fat, but I did it. Simon weighed in at 9 ½ lbs and of course I got my choice of names and chose Simon Paul.

Roy was so proud of his first son Brendan and likewise with Simon, indeed he was proud of all of his kids. But then a year later I fell pregnant again with a daughter whom we called Sarah, after my friend Ray from Kinning Park. Sarah was Ray's real name. It was around that time we had received bad news from Alan, Gussie's husband, Ray's uncle. He had come over to tell us but had written the news on a piece of paper and slipped it into Roy's hand. I watched him as he read, his face changing as he processed the information and asked,

'What's that?'

He told me that Ray was in a bad accident with her new partner Bob McCosh. It was a very bad winter that year with terrible black ice. Their car had skidded into another car and then rolled over. Everything happened so fast Bob didn't notice that Ray had fallen out of the car, during which time the car had swung round and rolled over again landing on top of Ray killing her instantly. Fortunately, Bob survived and none of the kids were in the car. Both Roy and I were devastated. I couldn't make it to the funeral – even the thought of it I found too horrific.

Three months later baby Sarah caught a cold which developed into Pneumonia. She died because of it. I was told it was a cot death. Both Roy and my problems seemed to stem from then on. I started drinking too much. Roy's health wasn't good. I was always having stones in my kidneys. There was never enough money. Things were very low then.

When Roy wasn't working, I would get a job, although women weren't paid very well at that time. It was usually a shop or a food place where I would help myself to food or clothes. I'd then go on to the amusement arcade. It was prize bingo with vouchers to spend on food, then on to the fish and chip shop, everyone ate so well! But of course, it didn't last long because Roy would start back to work, until one of his illnesses cropped up again.

I spiralled into a bad depression. I think it's called post-natal depression. I went to the doctors but was just told I had to put up with it. We called it baby blues. only now we know that it's quite a serious condition.

As soon as I realised things were bad with me and Roy I couldn't cope, well, I wasn't coping. We couldn't pay the bills, or the rent and I seemed to be constantly pregnant. After Sarah

I fell pregnant again. I didn't want another baby, so I asked my doctor for a termination – he refused.

At the time Roy got involved with his pal Rideout, who had become a Jehovah's witness. Roy began showing a keen interest in Rideout's religion. I was quite shocked with Rideout because it seemed every woman was chasing him; and he thought he was God's gift to women.

I put it down to a phase Roy was going through, but it turned out he was really interested in it. I wasn't happy about it because even though I wasn't a good practicing Catholic, I still called myself a Catholic. This all happened around the time that Sarah died. I blamed them for bringing evil into the house. They even brought a projector and screen so the kids could watch films of their teachings and lives in America. We didn't have a television and the kids loved it.

I used to go out to the bingo - Roy had to make sure that they were away before I got home. We never discussed it but one day Roy said he needed money to buy their books. I was adamant, that he pay for them himself. Bren went with his dad to the Kingdom Hall meetings a couple of times, but I don't think he really liked going. He only went because his dad asked him.

About this time, I had started to become unwell and realised I was threatening a miscarriage. I went to the doctors and the doctors said I would have to have a termination

When I told Roy he wouldn't have it. Doctor Smith came to see us and explained how serious the situation was. I had already told Doctor Smith Roy's beliefs; that Jehovah's Witnesses do not hold with termination. In the end Roy refused to sign the papers for me to have the termination leaving Doctor Smith no option but to advise Roy that he didn't need his permission because it was a life-threatening situation. I didn't have a termination, I miscarried anyway.

Things were always ringing in my head like Catholics are not allowed to prevent their wives from getting pregnant, in the past my mother was always saying little quips like that. I wasn't a good Catholic and heaven forbid, I couldn't get sterilized because it was considered to be a mortal sin. Your body is not for pleasure only for your husband to get you pregnant. I always believed and heeded what my mother said to me, even when we lived in Corby, she told me.

When I went to confessions on a Friday night to give the priest a note from her asking for £5 as she was a diabetic and couldn't take her insulin because there was no food in the house, and she had to have something to eat first. He always gave it to me – she would write in the note 'and please say a prayer at Mass on Sunday for her because she was ill.' I was also instructed to light a candle for her. I didn't have a penny for a box, but she said I didn't have to pay because the priest knew we were poor.

When I worked in the shops, I was allowed to help myself or supply them with whatever and she would say that's why the wages are so low because they know you help yourself. I believed her. I was so naïve back then.

My sister Louise was the only one I could turn to – she always bought the kids lovely clothes and toys at Christmas. She was always treating me, gave me all her clothes when she was finished with them as we were the same size. I had noticed her eating habits, when at work she only ate a cheese roll and a bowl of cornflakes at home in the evening. She was fixated about her figure.

She was very fit, walked everywhere. I didn't think too much of it at the time. Roy was out of work, and I had taken up a job in a baker's shop and café. I loved it and of course I could bring food home. The kids loved it too. Cakes and rolls, sausage rolls, pies every night. The bakers even made their own dumplings which were much appreciated too.

Great Yarmouth day trip – 1967/8

We couldn't afford many day trips to the seaside. I had five kids by then. Simon was the youngest and about four years old at the time.

We were all sitting on the beach enjoying the day and watching the donkeys move up and down. Then, in a split second, Simon wandered off the beach. Panic stations set in. The Police were called, and everyone was shouting his name. The beach was really busy. At the time Simon used to call me Jock largely because all mums friends called her that. Everyone was shouting 'Simon,' and then I heard walking along the front, a voice shouting out, 'Jock, Jock.'

I could see him on top of a man's shoulders. A couple had found him. The husband told me later, we asked him his mummy's name and he answered 'Jock,' the man thought I must have been foreign.

Then Simon started shouting, 'Jock, Jock.'

He could tell the couple his address as plain as anything; 67 Linden Avenue – all my kids were taught their name and address from an early age, just in case.

I thanked everyone for their help and then we went back to the beach and got ready and went for a pokey hat (ice cream). Tina got hers first, walked away and spotted a pound note on the ground. She brought it to me, 'Mam, look what I've just found!'

I said there's one thing were going to do with it is have us a fish supper; I naughtily added, 'God must have sent that to us for finding Simon again after his fright.'

It was a treat for all of us. Thank you, Great Yarmouth, for a memorable day.

The Pear Tree, Kettering – 1970

Poor wee Bev, because she was the eldest, she got it in the neck all the time, like when the Mr and Mrs Royal, the next-door neighbours. Mr Royal was lovely, a Council gardener, but Mrs Royal was a dragon, always moaning about the kids going into her garden, picking her flowers. But there wasn't anything in place to stop them getting in, no fence, nothing.

They also had a big pear tree in the back garden which hung over into our garden. I warned the kids not to climb it – she would have kittens, she didn't like animals either, so children and animals were a no-go. Then one day Bev's uncle Chris, who was the same age as Bev, around eleven years, made her climb the pear tree and she got stuck. Her knickers got caught and there she was shouting for help.

I looked out the upstairs window and was horrified to see what was happening. I ran down screaming like a banshee.

Chris bolted.

I was wearing wooden Scholl sandals and threw one at Chris and one at Bev. It landed on her head. I was more worried that Mrs Royal had seen and heard and made Bev apologise – but Mrs Royal hadn't even seen it. So Bev always remembers that I shopped her, she even remembers how heavy the Scholl sandals were – amazing eh!

CHAPTER 11

Things fall apart

Gradually things between myself and Roy started getting worse. One day Louise turned up at my work, it was around the Easter holidays. She asked if I would like to go up to Scotland for a week and that she would pay. I jumped at the chance but had to run it past Roy first. He was fine with it, two of my daughters went back to Scotland with the crowd that came down to visit. I remember sitting up all night waiting for them to arrive.

Originally the understanding was that nine of them were going to Gussies in Corby, but the number turned into fifteen with the possibility of more.

Isabel had won two thousand pounds at the bingo and was treating them for a weekend. Gussie had sent Alan, her husband in to tell me they couldn't stay with them as they were going up to Scotland. Tut, tut Gussie. She sent in dishes and bedding and other things to help and somehow word was sent to them to come down to us.

Ella, my sister was working in a club in Ferguslie at the time. I think it was called the Fergus, she said she would travel after she finished work. Having stayed up nearly all-night waiting for their arrival I had fallen asleep on the couch. Roy came downstairs opened the curtains and said, 'Is someone moving in or out in the street?' It was only a small cul de sac, I would have known if they were. Outside there was a big furniture van, I realised it was them and for a minute thought they had brought me some furniture.

Three men got out of the front seats. I recognised them all, John McVey, Ella's husband, Tam, their son, and cousin Thomas Irvine. Then they opened the back doors of the van, and I don't know to this day how many people and kids jumped out the back. The kids were running all over the street screaming with excitement. Then they bought in with them all their bags of food, square slice, tattie scones, scotch loaves – all the things we loved.

Some of the women had rollers in their heads and were wearing their pyjamas. They didn't care. They were from Feegie. They had put mattresses down in the van so everyone could get a sleep. There wasn't enough room in our house, so all the boys and men slept in the van. It was hilarious. We had a great weekend.

When they left, Tina and Alison wanted to go back with them, and Roy allowed it. Soon after myself, Louise, Bren, and Simon went up to Scotland to stay with Isabel and her son John. We went to bingo first then came home with a carry out of drink and ordered a curry for everyone including the kids. A party started up and later we heard raised voices coming from outside.

Isabel recognised one of the voices as that of her brother David, arguing and fighting with the lads from up the street. It never really came to anything, but the next morning Louise announced that she was going home because she didn't like being around what was going on including the drinking and partying; she wasn't used to any of that, it frightened her. I wasn't for going home, I was enjoying it. I thought it was great and stayed on a bit longer.

After two weeks I still wasn't ready for going back but after another week the kids wanted to go home. Tina wanted to take Bren and Simon back as they didn't want to stay any longer. Both the boys had a dark complexion. One time they had been out playing and got a bit lost, they went to the wrong house – all the paths and houses looked the same. When they knocked on the door a lady answered, and Bren and Simon told her they were looking for their mum. Naturally they spoke in very polite English accents. The lady shouted back into the house 'Does anybody know these two boys' mother?' She asked them what their mother's name was and when they said Josie, she knew it was me. Later I was told that she thought they were two Asian boys P.... – we all laughed at that.

Tina took the boys home on the Sunday and Alison stayed with me. Another couple of weeks went by and I didn't want to go back to Roy. We spoke on the phone, and I told him I wasn't coming back, and I was sending Alison home as I thought it was for the best. I decided I would put my name down for a house for the kids to come and stay with me – but it wasn't as easy as that.

I had started drinking heavily and getting into trouble with the police. A crowd of us were shoplifting and earning loads of money and partying all the time. I had beautiful clothes didn't want for anything. I sent money down for the kids and parcels of clothes, but Roy and I had stopped talking to each other.

My health started to suffer. I found a lump in my breast and was drunk when I phoned Roy to tell him. He asked me to come back – my drinking and getting into trouble with the police was getting worse. I hated myself and was getting more and more depressed and felt guilty being separated from the kids. I knew I was no good to them in that state.

I went to the doctors and was sent straight to the hospital. Several days after that I was admitted and had the lump removed. It took a week for the results. It was good news – all clear. And what did I do with that, I went out and celebrated.

By then, Roy and I had decided that we were better separated. Unbeknownst to me, he had filed for a divorce - I couldn't blame him. I had met someone else and so had he. I hadn't spoken to the kids for a while; they didn't have a phone, not many people did. I had to make arrangements for them to be at the phone box at a certain time. Only Alison and Simon would come to the phone to speak to me. I was left thinking that Bev, Tina, and Bren didn't want to speak to me, but they were teenagers and preferred to go out with their mates.

I much regretted that time and was ashamed of myself. I missed the kids terribly and kept thinking it was too late to fix things. I was told that Roy's girlfriend had moved in, and the kids didn't like her. I recall Simon telling me he put a laxative in her tea and thought it hilarious.

I was still living with Isabel when the fella I was seeing asked me to move in with him. He told me that the kids could come and stay in the holidays. He had a nice clean house, even did all the cleaning, cooking, and washing himself. I thought this was great, that things were going to change but a couple of days later the police came to search his house and arrested him for breaking into a club a few days before. I couldn't believe it. Money and drink were stolen. He went to court and got six months in prison and told me that if anything was to happen to him, I was to stay in the house and look after it until he got out.

I started to get things straight and made plans for the kids to come and stay but given the rent wasn't getting paid the Council soon wanted the house back. My fella pleaded with me to pay the rent until he got out. I tried explaining to the Council that he was in prison but they were determined to take the house back and so I was left to empty it. He wasn't happy about it, and I had to leave. We stored his things in another empty house next door to my nephew, but the Council got to it and removed it all.

I was back staying with Isabel and ended up back on the drink, partying, and shoplifting. When my fella got out of prison, we went to stay with his brother Charlie who only had a one bedroomed house in Thrushcraigs. Charlie always slept on the couch, and we had the bedroom. He wasn't very nice to Charlie; always shouting and bullying him, he was drinking heavily too.

I'd put my name down for a house – he was telling where to apply for but not Ferguslie. Added to which I found out I was pregnant. I was scared to tell Roy and the kids. I didn't know what to do so I just kept quiet.

I was always getting shouted at when he came home drunk – that I lost him his house, that I must have sold his furniture. I even had to stop him hitting Charlie a couple of times. I used to think I could handle myself but when he slapped me things started to get progressively worse. I should have got out of there. Charlie told me more than once to get away, but I didn't know him that well – it was the drink.

There were times when Charlie would clear off down to London to see his pals. During that time, I decorated his house, put in new carpets and curtains. I was about five months pregnant and had stopped drinking – but things were strained, he was out drinking more and more. I also found out that he was out drinking with his ex-wife. He would always claim it was her coming to the pubs where he drank, that there was nothing to it because she had remarried. By the time I'd reached six months I had started bleeding.

When I went to the hospital, they told me that the baby had died, and I would have to deliver the baby myself. I became very unwell and had to call an ambulance, he was drunk of course, too drunk to come with me. I was given an emergency section and delivered a baby boy who was still alive. I was groggy at the time and was asked to sign a consent form to be sterilized. They told me that the baby had to be taken to Yorkhill hospital in Glasgow as his lungs weren't fully developed and he was very underweight. He weighed in at 2 lbs.

I was put into a single ward in front of the sister's room and at about six o'clock the phone rang, and the sister came in and told me that the baby had died. A short while later she came back with the phone and said, 'Its Tina for you.' I burst into tears but managed to speak to her. Isabel had told them I was in hospital, so she phoned straight away.

I was so upset, not solely about the baby's death but all the shame and guilt came rushing into my head. What I had put my kids through. Tina told me not to worry about anything, that it was all in the past. I don't know if I was crying about the baby or the kids – possibly both?

Roy was so understanding, telling me everything would be okay. I stayed in hospital for three weeks because my scars weren't healing very well. The night before I was leaving, I sneezed, and the wound opened again which meant I had to go back into surgery for more stitches.

I hadn't seen the fella for days. He wasn't happy about the time I had been kept in hospital and was always drunk when he visited. Sometimes he would come up to the hospital drunk, shouting up to the window 'Josie, come home.' The nurses had to get security to get rid of him – they knew all about him and what he was like by then.

I was to get home again and was put in another ward for a couple of days with all the other women and their babies. He didn't visit for a few days. I phoned his cousins wife to let him know I wasn't getting home and to ask him to bring my clothes up. The hospital had arranged the baby's funeral. I didn't attend – he was buried in the remembrance garden.

I waited all day for him to bring my clothes, visiting hours had passed. I cried all through it. Then I phoned his cousins wife and told her that he hadn't come. I had to get out. It was Sunday and I knew he would appear later drunk. Maureen, the cousin's wife told me not to worry and that she would get some things together and come and get me. She took me back to her house. I had a shower and got into my nightie while she made dinner. We were sat watching the tele and she had the fire up full and kept asking me if I was comfy and whether I needed anything. I was feeling so hot and was sweating profusely. I thought I was resting my hands on my stomach then Maureen looked down and noticed I was bleeding through my nightie.

'Oh God,' I shouted.

The wound had opened again. An ambulance was called, and I was taken back to hospital.

He didn't even know that I had been out, stayed at Maureen's and then taken back in. He arrived at about midnight, drunk, shouting and swearing. The Police were called and took him away. I don't know what happened to him, I was too ill to be bothered. I had to stay in for another two weeks. The hospital had to hide me in a single room further up the corridor to protect me from him.

CHAPTER 12

Hair we go again

A couple of hair events have already been referred to in this book, but I felt it necessary to mention a few more.

The first time something happened with my hair I was about seven years old and in care with the nuns at Smyllum Park Orphanage when Sister Louise had cut my hair off with a big pair of scissors.

We didn't have tongs or straighteners in those days, so I would put the poker in the fire and curl my hair with that like a bubble cut – the number of times I burnt my fingers and singed my hair!

I was pregnant with my third daughter Alison and one of my cravings when carrying her was coal dust. Russels coal chirls, dust at the bottom of the wee bags of coal, my mouth watered every time I saw a bag. My mother would save me the dust.

One day I was going to the Barras, and I took an envelope full of dust with me. I sat on the bus dipping my finger in the envelope like I was eating sherbet and oh I was loving it. Then I noticed my reflection in the window, my mouth, lips, and chin were black. I didn't have a tissue or hankie and had to get off the bus. I made it worse by trying to wipe it off and got some funny looks.

Some friends of Bridies lived round the corner, Aggy and Joanie (his real name was John, but we called him Joanie as a nickname) and she asked me to bleach her hair one day. They had a narrow kitchen, and the living room was tiny. We sat by the fire while, Aggy on one chair and Joannie on the couch. I put the lotion on her hair and suddenly the lum went on fire, throwing soot all over us. I turned to Joanie, he just sat there with his tea in his hand and his fag in his mouth. He couldn't move. All of us sat there with soot on our faces, heads, and hair and when we saw his face we couldn't stop laughing because he had got the worst of the blast in his face. It was hilarious. We just carried on having a wee drink as if nothing had happened and abandoned the hair

We ended up in Kettering and moved into our own house – my hair was growing again after a couple of years. I was washing the floors and had a casserole in the oven. I could smell gas and realised that the gas was going out, so I went to get a coin for the meter and returned to washing the floor. After a while I could still smell gas and realised that it had completely gone out and needed relit, so before relighting it I decided to have myself a wee fag. I picked up a box of matches and without thinking, struck a match, lit my fag and opened the oven door. Bang!

All my hair at the sides and on top singed, my eyebrows, face, lips, and chin all burnt and blistered. I used to have a wee mastoid, not just a plook, on my chin nearly every month and no matter what I did, I could never get rid of it. However, the accident got rid of it right down to the root – after nearly fifty years, it never came back.

I should have gone to the hospital; I was in shock and the kids were due back from school. Bev was the first back and I had to go to bed. My sister Louise came round, and Bev explained what had happened.

Louise shouted up the stairs 'Do you want me to cut the burnt bits out?' then she came up to see me.

There I was sitting in bed, 'Cut what hair?' I spoke. 'I've no hair left!'

Louise had to go to the chemist to get some cream for my face. It took weeks to clear up. Thankfully after a few months my hair slowly started to regrow. I could never afford to go to a hairdresser back then and my hair was at a length that I couldn't do anything with it.

A new hairstyle came out called the Pixie Look. It was very short, two of my pals Colleen and Val had it so I thought why not. So, I started cutting my hair, I got right up in front of the mirror in my living room, scissors in hand, but it ended up getting more uneven as I continued to cut. I wasn't right so once again I ended up having to use smaller rollers in my hair and wear a headscarf for days at a time because I didn't want Roy to see what a mess, I'd made of it. During the time everyone wore their rollers and headscarves everywhere.

I ended up having to tell him what I'd done. I don't think he'd really noticed much of a difference, largely because he had probably seen me wearing the rollers and scarf for ages.

All he said was, 'I prefer you with your hair long!'

My three daughters had lovely thick hair and I vowed never to cut their hair, ever, and I never did.

Louise treated me to the hairdressers for my birthday, she suggested a perm. Her hair was always perfect because that's what she had. I didn't know what happened to your hair when you had a perm but went ahead.

When the hairdresser took the curlers out, I was left with these tiny wee curls – I didn't like it, but then I thought I'll wash that out when I get home, so I told the lassie to leave it and went home. So, when I got home, I washed my hair and put my rollers back in. I wanted my straight hair back. Louise popped in to see me after a week and asked

'Didn't you go to the hairdressers?'

I told her I did but didn't like it and so washed it out because it was too curly. She laughed and said, you must go each week to get a blow dry, but I didn't, I just carried on using my rollers. I was very naïve back then.

After another three kids my hair was back to normal, but that was when things weren't going well between me and Roy and eventually we split up. I ended up in Scotland. Late one night I found myself at my nephew, Peter's house. I had been drinking heavily. He was in the process of putting highlights in for a pal of his and I happened to mention that I'd always wanted to try them so he said he would do mine too. He applied the bleach and the rubber cap and told me not to fall asleep – we all did.

I woke up through the night with the cap still on my head annoying me. I pulled it off and went to the toilet. There was a large mirror next to the loo. I was still a bit drunk and got a shock. There I was sitting on the toilet, and I turned and looked into the mirror. My hair! It was still short at the time but had turned cotton wool white. I looked like a punk rocker. 'Jesus Christ, what have they done to me!'

Everyone was rolling about in hysterics.

Peter later said, 'Ya idiot, I told you not to fall asleep, you daft so and so.'

To make matters worse he phoned everyone, family, friends and neighbours. They flocked round to have a look at the new punk rocker on the block.

He gladly announce to them all, 'Well, I told you not to fall asleep!'

I was the talk of the steamie for ages after.

I had to send out for toners which didn't work. This involved getting in touch with my hairdresser friend Lorraine, to come down and tell me what to do. She came down, laughed her heid off and then snipped even more off, it ended up I got a darker dye on my hair.

Once again, I had the Pixie look, but all the chemicals had seriously damaged my scalp. I had to go the hairdressers on a regular basis after that because my hair was so short, I couldn't put it in rollers. I wore short hair styles all the time. One of the hairdressers I went to made a comment saying it was very thin on top. I was offended and walked out never to go back there again. Her remark really dented my confidence.

I started going to other hairdressers and would state upfront, 'Yes, I know my hair is thin on top, but need advice on how to handle it now.' I kept my hair very short and went every week to get it done properly. They advised me on everything which to this day I am very grateful for.

About seven years ago I developed breast cancer and again, lost my hair. Two years ago, I got the all clear, thankfully, but my hair has never grown in on top properly since.

Future Pathways have supported me these past couple of years on account of being a survivor of child abuse while in care at an orphanage. They helped me by paying for a couple of wigs. The cost of these wigs is around £400-700 each. I kept my hair very short while wearing the wig then suddenly my hair started growing again, so I tried on occasions to go without a wig. I would back comb my hair on top and pin it up which worked okay sometimes but at least it's my own hair – this has helped me regain my confidence. I don't know how I've got any hair growing back after all these episodes.

Someone once asked me if I would like to go to a musical called 'Hair' – yes, it was a joke.

My last hair episode was not with my hair, but one of my wigs. It was coming up for my sister Louise's seventieth birthday. She had just retired from her job. My daughter asked if I could get a big banner made for her workmates to stand behind. So, I ordered it and was due to collect it on the Saturday. My friend Georgie and I usually go to the bingo on Saturday afternoons, so we got the bus to the town centre and went to get off at the stop outside Gabriel's pub. It was really bad weather at the time, torrential rain, and high winds. Georgie got off first and as I was just about to step off when there was a huge gust of wind.

I was in the process of saying, 'God, the shop's shut,' and my wig flew off and disappeared like tumbleweed right into a puddle. The whole pavement was riddled with puddles and the wind was so strong that it blew the wig along through *all* the puddles.

Georgie ran into the pub leaving me standing before a bunch of men hanging about outside having a smoke. Speechless all they could do was look on with this shocked, bemused look on their faces.

All I could see was my wig getting blown mercilessly along the pavement.

Four young lads were heading towards me on their way to the football. When they spotted my wig on its travels they doubled over laughing and one of them shouted, 'Get the phones out!'

There was also a lady and her son walking towards me in the other direction – she was shouting, 'I'll catch it for you Mrs.'

Then someone else shouted from their car, 'Is that yer cat?'

Someone else bellowed back, 'It's her wig!'

All the traffic was at a standstill.

'No, it's my wig!' I shouted. I looked round and across the road there was a bus parked with passengers in it. Everyone was on their feet looking at what was going on.

The guys outside the pub said, 'Sorry missus for laughing but that was the funniest thing we've ever seen.'

Then the woman kindly brought the wig back. It was dripping wet. I thanked her, shook the wig and arranged it on my head while looking in the pub window. Then I turned to the guys and said, 'Is that okay? Is it on straight?'

They couldn't say anything for laughing.

I had to go into the pub and get Georgie out. We went on to the bingo and she ran in kidding me that she needed the toilet, but really it was to tell everyone what had happened.

Even the caller called down from the stage, 'Josie, mind you keep your hair on!'

I never heard the last of that, so that's why I don't wear my wigs in bad weather now.

The guys said it had made their day to which I replied, 'Well that's good, just as long as I've made your day.'

That's why I'm thankful for my own hair growing in. I love hats too, so that's my excuse.

CHAPTER 13

The kids

Before Simon started school we would always sit and watch all the children's programmes at 1.30pm. I had to do all the voices and movements as well as singing along with Simon. I really looked forward to that time each day.

Then one day, while waiting for one of them: Camberwick Green, Postman Pat, Fireman Sam, Bill and Ben, the Wooden Tops and Andy Pandy – I loved them all and still do, I don't think I've ever really grown up - Simon said 'Let's play a game of pirates. I'll tie you to the chair.'

Of course, I was game for it and allowed Simon to tie me. Then he went to the kitchen for a knife to use as a sword. He was holding it to my throat, growling as a pirate would do when our black cat, who was sitting at the back of my chair, pounced on Simon scratching him. He got such a fright and shouted, 'You black C...'

I think we all got a shock. I had never heard that word used in my house ever. I don't know where he picked it up from.

I shouted, 'Simon, that's a bad word!'

He replied, 'I never said that I meant you, bad cat.'

He could tell I was angry, and I made him untie me.

Poor Simon used to take wee fits; I didn't know why. I used to take him to the doctor and made appointments for the hospital, but they couldn't find anything wrong. Sometimes kids go through things and grow out of them. Tina used to do it as well. It was when she cried, she held her breath. I would just hold her until she was fine, and she soon grew out of it, but it wasn't until the kids were all grown up that you find out the truth.

Tina and the other kids would give Simon an ice lolly and because it was ice, he would lose his breath. Tina told him she would get all the kids to see Simon take a fit. It all came out one time when I was visiting. We were all sitting around having a laugh and wee stories would come out. I don't think Simon has ever eaten an ice lolly since. In fact, I think Tina said she used to charge the other kids to watch him take a fit. It was like a freeze shock he was having.

We went to Northampton Bingo, me Bev, Tina, Ali and another friend sometimes. And coming back they would always want to stop at the chip shop. Kerry had to back up to let in another car while we waited for Ali to get her chips. The other car happened to be the same make as ours.

She came out of the chip shop and jumped into what she thought was our car and said, 'No you didnae want any f..... chips.'

The driver replied, 'I didn't ask for any.'

Ali slunk out the car.

Tina's friend said, 'Quick, shout Ali.'

Tina said, 'No, leave her. See what happens.'

Ali slunk into our car saying, 'Did you see what I've just done?'

We were howling.

Another time, going to the same bingo, we were only ten minutes away and Ali had to have a pee. It was a moonlit night and she jumped into some bushes. She stripped off completely and started dancing about under the full moon. Unknown to her another car was parked up with a couple in it. They flashed their lights on Ali, she jumped back into the bushes, got dressed and got in the car. It was such a sight to see, she had us doubled over laughing.

One time Tina had fallen out with Darren and asked Bev to take her to withdraw Darren's money from the hole in the wall. While she was waiting for the cash Ali jumped into a trolly, took her top off and because they had been drinking started messing about so Tina joined Ali and did the same. When she finally went to get her cash from the machine it was declined then Bev happened to notice the big camera above but didn't let on because Tina had to go back the next day to retrieve her bank card.

Bren told me a wee story of when he and his dad took Simon to the fishing tackle shop to get maggots for the fishing trip they'd planned for the next day. The man in the shop knew them and went out into the back and came back with two apples. He gave one to Bren and said give the other one to 'your little sister'.

They howled.

Simon hadn't realised what he had said. Both he and his brother had long hair, it was the fashion back then. I don't know if Bren ever told him of the shop keeper's mistake. I love reminding the kids of some of the funny stories relating to them.

Trips with Bev and Tina

My first ever holiday abroad and flying was around 1984 when I flew to Yugoslavia. I wasn't keen on it, but I've since been to Benidorm a few times with friends from Gallowhill and a few times to Turkey and Australia, although the latter is too long a journey. They were good times, especially visiting the steam baths and the best laugh was the jeep.

Bev and Tina came on that holiday. Two jeeps and team water fights between us, but the best was Tina and a friend of ours, John, who was gay, convincing them to go on the donkeys. The donkey owner slapped the donkeys on the backsides, and they took off with both Tina and John disappearing into the distance screaming, 'Mam, Mam.'

We were all in stitches, she's never got over it.

When we got back to the hotel, my room was on the ground floor and the first to be reached. Now usually I'm the first to race for the toilet but that time everyone was in before me. John thought Tina was going into the toilet first, so he jumped into the toilet and hid behind the shower brandishing a huge knife.

Instead, it was Bev who ran in shouting, 'is it free?' Not getting an answer, Bev ran in with no time to lock the door. No sooner had she done so when that mad devil John pulled the shower curtain back and raised the knife – he was also wearing someone's dress and a long blond wig for effect.

Bev screamed and froze at the same time; the reception desk was outside my bedroom and all the Turkish boys came running in to see what all the screaming and laughter was about only to be confronted by that idiot John dressed as a mad blond and Bev transfixed to the loo.

Bev and Tina took me to Magaluf for my 70th birthday as a surprise. They didn't tell me until they got me to the airport and I found out where I was going. It was really good fun. I think I was the oldest person there. The flight attendant was a young guy and Bev and Tina ordered champagne, he was great fun and said to me, 'You know where you're going madam?'

I said yes as Magaluf has a rather rude nickname and he said, 'I hope I'm on your return flight.' He was, and we all had a great laugh on the way back.

We also travelled the Blackpool several times – always at the new year. We love that time. I haven't been for a few years. My nephew Peter always came with us. Sometimes he would drive me there and we would go to the bingo first then on to the pub or club. The first one he took me to was called The Flying Handbag. I didn't know it was a gay bar. Two lads were kissing at the pool table, and I said 'Peter, look at they two.'

A crowd of girls sat down next to us, everyone was friendly and Peter said, 'Yes Josie, it's a gay bar!'

Again, it was great fun.

When my brother Tam died, we travelled down to Birmingham where he had lived. His local pub arranged most of the funeral wake. They were very lovely – in the men's toilet there was a big barrel full of something; I noticed people were going in and helping themselves to the contents so me being nosey went over to have a look and picked some of these things out of the barrel.

I didn't know what it was and showing them, said to Peter, 'What are these?' Stupid me!

Peter looked at me with a stifled smile and said, 'They're condoms.'

Well, my mouth fell open!

Again, I hadn't cottoned on it was a gay bar and that was how we realised that Tam was gay too. They were all the best people I have ever met – they even put a drag show on for Tam that continued throughout the day and all night. Drag queens came from all over Birmingham in his honour. What a send-off they gave him – everyone said how much they loved Tam. We'll never forget them.

Tam had been in the army for 22 years and they said Tam had helped loads of kids off the street and homeless and managed to get them help. I think the pub was called The Village. I'd like Peter to take us back there one day. I lost touch with them because my ex-partner died, my sister Ella, who was Peter's mum, and May, all died within months of each other.

My sister Bridie is in a care home in Glasgow now. It was supposed to be a temporary arrangement but lately she hasn't been keeping too good. She can't help herself very well now so I think it will be more permanent. She'll be ninety-one this year. Out of fifteen in our family there's only four still alive. These last three years have been awful for everyone, and our family has lost many close family and friends as is the same for a lot of people. I hope this year will be better and healthier for us all.

Something has just come on the television about the war which had ended on the 15th of August 1945, just two days before I was born. It was called VE day and it brought back what my mother told me about that time she had been talking to a priest and they went their separate ways and shortly after a bomb dropped and the priest was killed. My mother said it was a miracle we all survived, and everyone mucked in to help the injured, she even found part of the priest's clothing. It must have been a terrible time. I couldn't imagine how bad it was.

Shenanigans

When Bev was in hospital in Italy, she was hallucinating a lot of the time. She recalls the four doctors tell her, 'Right what we have decided to do with your belly is that we are going to make it look like a Celtic dart board and then drew one on her belly.' It was one of the first things she checked when she came round. I was sitting on the chair in the corner at the time when I saw her frantically looking at her belly.

One of Bev's doctors was her beautician and waxed her top lip and eyebrows. At the time everyone was wearing these hats that she referred to as Hungarian hats, she had invented them. When she finally got out of the hospital all the shops and markets were selling them. Bev was shocked because she had thought she had dreamt it.

CHAPTER 14

Breast Cancer

I returned to live in Corby when Ali was diagnosed with breast cancer. I left my partner and moved to live with Ali and the children to support them. It was coming up to Halloween, so I decided, while waiting for my furniture to arrive, to have a housewarming party. I decorated the walls with bin bags, the ceilings too, cobwebs everywhere, hanging skeletons, spiders and horrible insects all over.

We had hotdogs, hamburgers and Halloween food and cakes. Ali had a big rocking chair. I dressed a couple of pillows and made a witch from them, sat it on the chair with false face, wig, cape, hat, the works using Bren's clothes and had a big black cat sat on its knee with a bottle of Buckfast sat at his feet. (Water in a bottle only). Everything looked great. The kids were encouraged to rock the chair, prod and muck about with the witch for a while, then followed the games: dookin apples and catch the treacle scone – blindfolded, which was hung on a string. I would smack their faces with the scone; I loved doing that. Then Bren changed into the witch and sat on the chair. He sat very still, and the kids were brought in for a story, which was Little Miss Muffet. I was tasked to tell it.

The kids were told not to touch the chair or the witch as it was sleeping. I started the story – just watching their entranced faces was a picture particularly when I dragged the story out by asking questions about their favourite things to do with Halloween, witches and ghools. Their answers were very interesting.

There was a large spider positioned just above my head ready to be lowered and thrown into the seated ring of children.

Then at a strategic point Simon appeared at the window dressed as Casper the Ghost and making all the faces. When he did so the kids started shouting, 'He's behind you!'

Then I would carry on telling the story very slowly.

All the grown-ups were standing about watching, revelling in the fun. Now Bren was waiting for me to get to a particular point in the story … when along came a spider. That was his cue to leap off the rocking chair screaming.

The kids got such a fright they started screaming.

Bren's daughter, two-year-old Shannon, jumped out of her mum's arms and landed with a crash on the floor. She ended up with a bump to her head but fortunately was okay.

All the kids continued shouting, 'Finish the story, finish the story.'

We couldn't carry on for a while because of the commotion. It was hilarious. We still laugh about that party even now. I'm glad the kids have remembered those days.

.oOo.

When Ali first got her diagnosis, we had made arrangements for having a fund-raising event. Ali wanted to get involved and wanted to lose weight along with my sister Gussie in aid of Cransley Hospice. It was our local cancer hospital. They did a great job there – people were always raising money for them.

Ali started her chemo and was advised that she may lose her hair and to consider having her hair cut short so that way it wouldn't be such a shock. She had her hair cut short, but they didn't advise her to go on a weight loss programme.

So, we all had some fun fund-raising events and one special one was for her and the kids to go to Disney World in Florida. She was told it wasn't advisable as it would be too much so instead, she decided she wanted to visit Ireland. She loved Ireland, but a short time later she lost her lovely hair.

She phoned me one morning to say, 'Mam, it's started.'

I told her I'd be down shortly. I had recently bought Ali a little square scarf just in case she felt embarrassed. I had seen other girls wearing them as bandanas and very nice too.

She had to go to the Post Office for her benefits and had to cross through a square in the town centre. She was feeling very apprehensive in case she met anyone she knew. Ali was so well known where she lived in Corby. She decided to try walking over herself but wanted me to watch her.

She started walking and as she got to the end she turned round and went into a fit of laughing, thumbs up. I went to her and told her that the worst part was over. She was fine after that, coming out of the Post Office was a group of friends, they had a chat, and nobody even passed any comment. She was so brave.

I went to a couple of shops to get the address for the popular berets by Kangol and Nike, which she loved. I wrote letters to both company's but got the addresses mixed up and sent the letters to the wrong firms. Later I received letters back informing me what I had done but they sent me the hats anyway which was nice of them. Ali particularly loved the Kangol red beret and eventually Tina kept the beret as a keepsake. Later she started adding charity badges to it.

Ali had explained early on to her kids about her cancer and diabetes. Her kids were very good supporting her through her diabetes and knew when she was unwell. They helped her so much with her condition. Catherine, her eldest, was a typical teenager with her mood swings – Little Britain comes to mind, she can take 'Vicky Pollard' off to a tee.

Corina was the exact opposite and Ciaran was just a toddler and they were all too young to fully understand their mum's illness, so their dad explained, and we all helped at the time.

Day trip to Largs

I remember telling Bev, Tina, and Ali a wee story just after their dad died - I was coming back to Paisley and had to change trains at Birmingham New Street Station. I was still a bit upset about having to leave the kids so soon after losing their dad. I sat on some pipes crying and upset thinking I would like to go to Largs for the day. I don't know what made me think of that, but I often did that in the past to get out of his way and usually made me feel a little peaceful and better. So a few days later I went to Largs.

I walked up to my old home 'Barrholm' and knocked on the door. A lovely lady answered. I asked if I could look around, but she said it wasn't possible because it was now an old people's home, and she closed the door. So, I nipped round the back to the playground and sun house where we played. I took some photographs; it was so nostalgic. I left passing by the huge front gate and when I looked back, I noticed the big wrought iron sign with cherubs on the top was missing. That was sad because I had some happy memories there.

I walked down Nelson Street, got to the bottom and there was a little antiques shop. It was closed and I peered through the window looking at the brass things and suddenly a little voice made me jump.

It said, 'I also love looking in these wee shops.'

When I looked it was an old lady, she was tiny with long white hair brushed back.

We got talking and I told her why I was in Largs that day. I told her about the kids' dad passing, that I felt really upset and a bit lost. She told me the story of her working in some big manor house as a thirteen-year-old with her mother. She had ended up pregnant with a baby. I think it was taken from her and she was sent away because it was the owner's child.

She went on to tell me, 'Anytime you come back to Largs you'll get me in that little charity shop across the road. I don't work there, but I'm in there every day for a cup of tea and a chat. Look me up, my name's Mary,' she said.

I told her my mother's name was Mary and that she was very small and at one time had long white hair which she wore in a bun.

I went back and visited the charity shop sometime later, but nobody had heard of Mary. She had also told me before Barrholm closed it was apparently partially destroyed. A boy had been smoking and the play hall went up in a fire – I later found out that was true.

After my operation

When I was in the hospital recuperating after the operation for breast cancer Bev and Tina had come up to support me. My doctor and his assistant, Alison, had come along to tell me what they were going to do and said they were going to put a tube into my hand with a blue dye. Joking I asked for green dye instead of the blue. The doctor didn't realise I was winding him up and apologised saying, 'I'm so sorry madam, we only do blue dye.'

We were in kinks laughing and his assistant had to explain to him we were having a joke relating to Celtic and Rangers – I think it went over his head and he didn't understand the joke properly. So, the day I had the operation, which went okay, I phoned Bev and Tina and asked them to bring along a green coloured wig for me. When the doctor and his assistant were doing their rounds, I put the wig on ready for when they arrived.

Tina shouted to the nurse, 'Can mum go to the toilet?

'Yes,' said the nurse.

'Can you give me a hand to help her up?'

Bev had her camera on standby ready to video the moment the doctor came by.

The moment he appeared I sat up, 'Doctor, I thought you said the dye wouldn't affect me.' His mouth dropped as he stared in disbelief.

The nurse told the doctor we were winding him up and then added with a wink that she was, 'throwing me out.'

The doctor took it well. Such a lovely doctor and he was also the one who was able to give me the *all clear* news adding, in the nicest possible way, that he didn't ever want to see me again.

I mentioned to him that the operation had left me with odd sized boobs, can't you do the other one?

He said, 'Don't tell everyone out in that waiting room that I've given you a boob job because they'll all want one.'

CHAPTER 15

Return to Feegie

Since I moved back to 'Feegie'- which I'm so glad I did, I've met so many friends old and new and found that they're friendliest folks and so helpful.

The Tannahill Centre is brilliant, all the events and learning and socialising, something for all ages, and help. The entertainment tributes nights to dance classes are brilliant. I try to join in most things and the help that is available is superb. You can also volunteer, and they all do a great job organising events.

I was recently asked to dress as the late Queen for her Jubilee and was very honoured to be asked to award each volunteer a certificate for their help and free time that they had given.

I learned so much back in the day in Feegie, all the old stories and sayings. I was told when kids went to the pictures on Saturday mornings, you could get in free if you bought a couple of jeelie jars (jam jars).

Go-karts, boys made them with four pram wheels and a plank of wood to sit on and string to guide it. It was their pride and joy.

Girls played beds, 'hopscotch,' or ropes but not when I lived in England. It was 1960 and Rock and Roll was out, that was my era and corner cafes.

Back in Feegie it was great with all your games and favourite sweets from the ice cream van, kids waiting patiently for the ring of the bells, running towards it. Porellis was ours with their empty ginger bottles – only on a Saturday night for us, a pokey hat, 'cornet,' penny caramel or highland toffee and making pom poms using the cardboard top off the milk bottle. Great pastimes and games and even mothers coming to play ropes with the kids. Those were the days.

Then there was the auld pully to dry your clothes, you'd raise it up to the ceiling, it was usually in the kitchen. A jawbox was a sink in a single end room, 'room and kitchen' or but and ben.

I still love all the auld sayings and I hear new ones every day. I laugh when I say them to my kids and hear them asking what they mean, as most of them are English.

I remember my granddaughter Catherine with Corina her sister and brother Ciaran came to visit me in Gallowhill. I sent her to the James' shop across the road in Dundonald Road. She came back saying, 'Nanna, the man in the shop speaks Scottish.'

I replied, 'Yes because James was born here.'

She was indignant, 'But he's black and he's Asian,' she gave me a confused look.

I couldn't help but laugh. I told her when I first moved to Kettering, I was called 'Jock' quite a lot by my friends and I thought that was great until I realised Kettering people didn't really like the Scots, especially our housing manager, a Miss Watson. She wasn't very nice, very strict. She had to come to visit us on numerous occasions, usually for rent arrears.

She was always passing comments, 'What, another baby?' and once she said, 'You really should go back to Scotland, where you come from.'

I was very upset and told my husband Roy what she said. He went mad and went to see her. I don't know what happened, but I never had any problem from her again, 'Auld Cow.' Now that's a figure of speech, no pun intended.

Back in the day, myself and nearly everyone in the family enjoyed drinking their tea from the jeely jar. You had to put a spoon in it first in case it cracked, but it was the best cup of tea ever, even Roy enjoyed it. We would take turns from it. I think that's where she passed the comment about going back to Scotland if I liked it so much because I was drinking my tea from a jar, and she commented I hadn't even got cups. The kids didn't understand that and one Mother's Day I received a lovely china cup and saucer, and Roy got a Father's Day mug. I still drink my tea from a china cup and saucer.

Dalskeith Crescent

During the first year of moving to Dalskeith Crescent in 2005, I had a Christmas party housewarming for family and friends. We had carol singing and the house and front garden were full.

My friend Louise dressed as Father Christmas and gave all the kids a selection box each. There were hot dogs, hamburgers, juices and of course, a wee swally for the grown-ups.

We had a competition for the loudest singer, a couple of parents were to judge. My sisters, Ella and Bridie were there too. They fair enjoyed themselves. It was so funny watching all the kids faces belting out the carols but of course, they weren't happy because I won – I reminded them that I used to be a bingo caller and my dad was a coalman. They weren't impressed, so I said, 'You're right, I shouldn't have been in it because it was my game.'

My next-door neighbour Cathy told me next day the priest visited her, and she told him what a great night we'd had and about the carol singing.

He said, 'Tell Josie, I'll be having the carol singing at her house from now on as that accounts for why there was hardly anyone at the chapel that night.'

Those get togethers still go on now. Last summer we all gathered round at my niece, Ashley's garden for a bingo night with all the families and neighbours on Saturday nights. Wednesdays it was held at my other nieces' house, Nikki. We all looked forward to them, that was when the lockdown was lifted.

Up until two years ago my very good friend June lived close by. June loved to party too. We had some great celebrations together and she doted on her kids and grandchildren, they were her world. June had suffered for several years with kidney failure and had had a kidney transplant a few years before she died. But that didn't seem to stop her from doing everything for her family; their washing, their meals, babysitting and running after her man Tam. She is so badly missed.

Then more tragedy was to follow when her brother Tam died some six months ago.

Tam was my pal, we were drinking buddies, we would also go to the bingo and the liberal club together. I once taught Tam to jive, even though he always claimed he had two left feet – we had a good laugh at that. Tam remembered Sylvia's husband from the Rosebud pub where he was the manager for a period. Tam was in one of the domino's teams. Both Ella and one of her sons, Peter worked there for a while but not at the same time as Stewart. His sister worked in the bookies across the road and Sylvia worked in the off licence round the corner in Well Street. Everyone used these places, so it is a wonder that we never knew anything. I believe they moved to London in 1986 so I think we must have seen each other back then. Isn't life strange and unbelievable.

Tam, like June is very much missed, he was much loved too. Like June he also suffered from kidney failure but was also a diabetic. He loved the horses and Celtic – his family miss him so much. They gave him a great send off, horses with green white and gold feathers and carriage and on his coffin was painted a scene from the racecourse – a really fitting tribute. I made a huge banner and collage of him and hung it on my garden wall as my house was the last house out the street. Everyone was also given little Celtic ribbons for their lapels and those in cars wore Celtic scarfs, the same was done for June's funeral.

Only months before we celebrated June's special birthday. Her kids had set up a table in the back garden and had a very fancy tea party and karaoke.

It was my 75th birthday two years ago and they all surprised me with the mobile bingo bus. We had a brilliant night with birthday cake, balloons, karaoke, and dancing in the street. Well done Feegie and the Tannahill Centre along with the Darkwood Crew for a kind and brilliant surprise – that's why I am very content and happy with my life now. My kids can see how content I am after such a long and terrible journey. The kids enjoy coming to Feegie on visits.

.oOo.

I am always looking for something to get into. I've always fancied joining a drama group, doing a bit of acting, I love comedy. I once saw a comedian on the news who had been brought up in care and had been abused and turned his life around by making fun of the treatment he had suffered while in care – making it a joke. I think he was very brave, and it worked for him, he was very funny and clever.

I have been in touch with Future Pathways who have helped and guided me in the past and they put me in touch with The Book Whisperers to help with writing my story. We have also spoken about a drama group. I hope I can do it - as everyone keeps saying to me, 'Josie, you should have been on the stage, yer aff yer heid.'

I tell them, 'No, I'm no, my psychiatrist always says to me no, yer no, Josie, it's all the dafties around you!' And yes, I've

94

had a few sessions with said doctors and counsellors when I got into trouble with the police and having bad flashbacks and drink related problems. But happily, that's all in the past and I try to deal with it in my own way and like that comedian, turn it around and see some of the funny things and just make people laugh.

It's good to hear friends at the bingo say, 'Josie, on party nights you make us laugh.'

Bev and Tina, Bren and Simon have a great sense of humour too.

I was in hospital about four years ago. I had a flare up of my medical condition, Crohn's Disease, it's not very nice and painful. Bev and Tina had come to visit me, I didn't know they were coming. My niece Nikki came into the ward first, she had a suspicious grin on her face and trying not to laugh she looked over to the door window. The girls had their faces pressed up against the glass. I could also hear bells ringing. They walked in and were dressed in Indian dancer outfits accompanied by the music 'Spirit in the Sky.' Some of the nurses and patients were howling with laughter and clapping – and they say I'm off ma heid!

So, any time friends or family are in hospital, I have to dress up and cheer them up.

When Nikki's dad, Ian, went into hospital and was feeling a bit better, his wife Isabel and his sister Helen asked me to dress up to cheer him up.

One night we brought him some wee bottles of stout and shared them with the other patients. I dressed up as Minnie the Mouse, singing and dancing like an idiot. A patient commented, saying 'Your auntie is dead funny,' and Ian replied, 'No she's not, she should be in the loony bin. She's off her heid!'

Sadly, Ian passed away and is very much missed – we go way back, Ian and Isabel stayed with us a couple of times in Kettering.

My sister May lived in Glasgow and on her 65th birthday we arranged a party for her. Gussie and her daughter Joan came through from Corby along with some nieces and Joan's daughter Natalie plus Ella, Bridie and her brother John. My son-in-law Jim got me a huge 4ft fake sponge cake all decorated. May was a very shy, nervous person but loved a get together and as a surprise for her I dressed up as Elvis with huge sideburns and a black wig.

The party was held in a pub next to May's house, she didn't drink but loved the company and was a regular. I had to get dressed outside the pub, making an entrance when the Elvis song played. I had brought a huge pair of bloomers with me, and Joan gave them to May to throw at me when I finished singing – she still didn't know it was me.

May threw the bloomers and I picked them up and showed them off shouting 'Whose are these? Are they yours May?' She was a wee skinny thing and all embarrassed shaking her head, 'Nooo.'

After a wee singsong I left to get changed and sat next to May. She turned to me and said, 'Josie, you just missed Elvis, he was singing to me.' I kept a straight face and said 'I'm sorry I missed him. So, it appeared, Elvis had left the building.

She will never know it was me.

May passed away some twenty years ago. I was with her at the time and a strange thing happened – her long-term partner, John, had also died sometime before. They were devoted to each other, and she missed him terribly. May had received the last rights and was very near the end when she suddenly sat up, shouted and pointed to the chair in the corner, 'John, I won't be long.' Then she lay back, closed her eyes and died soon after.

May had had a really hard life, especially with drink problems and ill health but with the help and support of Alcoholics Anonymous (AA) and John, she was able to get back on track.

May also had a son who I was told, was taken away from her by her partner's family. She never saw him again but often spoke to him – he lived in America. He was found a short time before she passed. He was found, I think by the AA and Salvation Army, but sadly she never got to see him. He stayed for the funeral and was a very nice, polite person. We exchanged a few stories, and he went home. He has phoned Gussie a few times since but not lately. Maybe it's for the best.

May told me once that we stayed in Gallowhill as children. I didn't know that, but when May visited me, she said she thought it was the same street, but they all look the same. It turned out the house was just round the corner from Dundonald Road where I was – the family lived in Gallowhill Road.

Lorraine

I used to go to my friend Lorraine's hairdressers and sit on the reception desk to answer the phone and book appointments just to pass my days and in return I received free hairdo's and just a 'little' beauty treatment. Little Stacey was the beautician and one Thursday evening, which was a late, half price night, she was with her last customer, when an Asian couple appeared and I had to ask Stacey, as it was quite late. She asked what they were looking for – it was the lady's eyebrows, so she agreed, but I was to lock the door and not let anyone else in.

The lady was in full sari dress and it was her husband who did all the asking as his wife couldn't speak any English. I hadn't realised how thick and heavy her eyebrows were. After Stacey had finished – and it took a lot longer, she explained to the husband it had to be full price, which was £7. He wasn't happy so Stacey let it go and only charged half price and didn't even get a tip for her trouble.

A short while later Bev and Tina were coming up to visit Paisley so I decided we'll wind Stacey up with a prank. I borrowed a sari outfit from an Asian friend's wife and Sharon, our other friend dressed and made Tina up. She had to hide in the toilet for a while until Stacey was free. All our pals were in the hairdressers at the time, it was a Saturday afternoon and we were about to close and have a drink.

Lorraine was tasked with informing Stacey that the Asian lady was back to have her eyebrows tidied up and because she was on her own without her husband, she agreed to do it.

Lorraine had led Tina on to the couch. Tina lay there with some hair that I had cut from a wig and placed on Tina's brows with a little cream. In the meantime, Stacey had gone and prepared the wax bowl then turned to Tina who flicked her brows and the hair skitted off. Stacey screamed and Tina sat bolt upright just in time to see the back of Stacey bolting through the door. Sharon was there with the video to capture the event, it was hilarious, poor Stacey.

Bruce

I was at the Globe Bingo one night with two young lads, now regulars, Drew and Ronnie. There is a connection because I know Drew's mam Janet, from Gallowhill. We started reminiscing about the times while living in Gallowhill. Drew was only a lad then, but he told us a funny story of how a group of lads would hide in the closes with thread stretched on to the pavement across the road.

They would wait for us to come out the pub, 'The Rocky,' and pull it up as a drunk walked towards it. It turned out that they did it to my ex and he fell over. You could hear all the kids howling with laughter. Yes, Drew was one of them and said all they could hear him shouting was 'Ya wee b…..'s. I know who you are and I'll get you tomorrow.' It was hilarious, particularly as nobody liked him.

We had a big Alsatian dog called Bruce. All the kids loved him, Bruce was probably with them too because when he saw him coming up the street he would bark to get out or otherwise he would be with the kids playing.

The next time I went to the Globe Bingo, I took them a photo of Bruce bringing me tea bags in his mouth. Drew especially loved Bruce, him and another wee lad were playing with Bruce, chasing each other when the lad fell, and Bruce grabbed him by the bottom of his trousers, but he must have bitten too hard and nipped his ankle. I was at the window watching them – the lad must have shown his mum.

He was taken to the hospital where they put a bandage round his ankle and gave him a jag. He came to the house the next day to play with Bruce. I asked him why he wasn't at school, and he said, 'Bruce bit me the night before and I had to go to hospital with me maw just in case.'

'Why didn't you come and tell me?' I asked and he said he said it was because he was okay.

A short time later I saw him and Bruce standing outside his close begging people for money. He had Bruce sitting next to him. When people asked what had happened, he would say, 'Bruce bit me but he didn't mean it, he's my friend.

I showed Drew the photo and he asked if he could keep it. 'Yes,' I said. So, he placed it on his table and won £500. I knew I wouldn't get the photo back after that.

I enjoyed living in Gallowhill in the early years, but once things started happening and the unit opened, people with drink and drugs problems moved in – that wasn't a good time.

My house got burgled three times. Everyone gradually moved away.

CHAPTER 16

College

I was glad to meet up with some old faces at the bingo, but I am so glad we moved back to Feegie. Before I moved back, I enrolled at the Reid Kerr College on a hair and beauty course, I had enrolled on it before and loved it.

When I phoned to enquire about the classes I told them I was over fifty and felt a bit old joining all the young ones. Was I being silly at my age? I just wanted to fill my days and have something useful to do. I was really interested in natural potions for the face. I never used soap on my face and still don't, so the classes were perfect for me. So, I enrolled and went to all the classes, I wasn't drinking then and was in good health, going for saunas every day. I loved it.

On the first day at the class the lecturer asked for a volunteer to lay on the couch for a demonstration. She was holding my arm straight up rubbing some lotion onto my arm when the door opened, and a wee man popped his head round the door.

He said, 'I'm from the Paisley Express paper. Can I interview you and a student?'

As I lay there, I was volunteered. Headline news a few days later read *Reid Kerr Student Josie takes it lying down*. It was very funny. The phone calls I got on that.

I finished the course and Bev helped me with my work; we used to practice for the exam. Bev said I'd be top of the class because I had done good.

The night before my exam finals, me, Peter and Ella went to the bingo. We had just turned onto the motorway when a woman driver, coming in the opposite direction bent down to pick something up out of her bag. She must have forgotten to stop and crashed into us. I ended up with a cracked knee, whiplash and my glasses fell off and I stepped on them. Ella and Peter both had whiplash and Ella dislocated her arm, so of course I couldn't carry on with my exams and that was the end of that.

When I first started the hair and beauty course, two of my nieces, Sarah-Jane and Andrea had signed up for the same course and, typical young ones, were full of giggling and tittering. The instructor, Fiona, knew me from way back because she was a hairdresser for a short while.

I'd missed part of the conversation because of Sarah-Jane and Andrea's carry-on and all I heard was Fiona say the word sex. I thought to myself, what has sex got to do with hair and beauty and so I asked Fiona, and everyone burst out laughing. What she actually said was it didn't matter what sex, male or female, as it was nearly the same procedure. I was so embarrassed and of course Sarah Jane, Andrea and myself, couldn't concentrate for the rest of the session.

Soon after that we had another fund-raising event for breast cancer. My other niece Nathalie had enrolled at another college for hair and beauty and was doing very well and later took a step up to Greenock College. Nathalie was keen to take part in the fund raiser.

My nephew Thomas volunteered to have a full body wax and Nathalie was glad to do it as it was for my daughter Ali and Nathalie and Thomas' cousins cancer fund raiser. Prior to this, Nathalie, bless her, had started doing homework and all her cousins and friends would go to her house. I went one night to have my eyebrows done. There was about half a dozen people waiting. We all sat nattering, having a cup of tea and having a good laugh. Nathalie had asked everyone what they were having done, but as I said, with all the joking and carrying on I said, 'Can we get started because I'm going to the bingo?'

I lay on the couch – I was also having a face cleanse. It was great lying on my back getting my face done, all relaxed – but as its Nathalie and family and friends, they never stop giggling and joking and of course gossiping. I was killing myself laughing with all the bits of gossip I was hearing; it was so funny.

Eventually Nathalie handed me a mirror, 'How is that?'

I looked in the mirror, 'Nathalie, you haven't done my eyebrows, they were to be waxed and tinted.'

She replied, 'Yes, I have touched up your eyelashes.'

We all burst out laughing and she quickly did my eyebrows, but Nathalie made up for it when she did the Ruby Wax on Thomas, thank you Nathalie for all the money raised.

CHAPTER 17

Making the connections

A few years ago, when I was in Gallowhill I got a call from Bridie saying, 'Josie, you need to tell our brother Eric to stop that nonsense and leave things alone.'

I wasn't sure what she meant at first but later realised she was referring to what we called our 'secret sister.'

When Bev was about two our mother kept calling her Sylvia which we all found odd. I asked maw, 'why do you keep calling Bev Sylvia?' and she whispered, 'It's a long story, I tell you one day.' Standing in the doorway was Bridie with a strange look on her face, so I knew there had to be a secret or some kind of gossip of some sort related to it. Bridie was forever telling me I was too nosey and not to ask too many questions.

I didn't get to the bottom of the Sylvia story until years later. Apparently, when the family were taken into care my mother had another baby which she called Sylvia but that was all the information that was given and none of the older family members ever spoke of her. But being the curious one I wasn't happy to just leave it there, also it niggled me that no one ever spoke about our father. I didn't ask any questions, and no one ever volunteered any information about him – I just thought it was a bit strange, but more on that later.

.oOo.

The street where we had lived had tenements; three up. We were in the middle and the second close into the street. My maw had the best view of the entrance to the street and gave everyone the nod when the electric, gas or police came.

Nearly everyone had broken into their meters or, if you were lucky, my mother would sell the key to the meters. She told me it was usually a penny.

She had this hat which she would wear to let people know. If it had a feather in the front, it meant gas. A feather to the back, electric. I don't know what she used for the police but granted they used to appear in a large van called the black maria.

I think ma maw was dabbling in a few things at the time. People helped each too. Ma maw often assisted the midwife, getting things in place, most people had home deliveries. There was an incentive because you got paid an extra £28 if you had your baby at home – that was a fortune. Ma maw told me once that she was waiting for the midwife and Dr Gilmore, nicknamed Conky Gilmore on account of his big nose, to arrive. It was also rumoured that he had a problem with the drink but that's another story.

Ma maw was trying to light the fire ready for hot water and warming the towels - everyone shared what they had, loaning towels and bedding for the deliveries. She had screwed up newspapers and was just getting the last sheet to put in front of the fire to draw the lum and get the fire going when it caught fire. Conky had already arrived and shouted through 'Are you there Mary McKenna?' Being resourceful my mother used her black skirt to draw the lum, she took it off and held it there not realising that it had singed and burnt the back side of the skirt. Conky noticed and said,

'Mary McKenna, did you know you have a hole in your erse?'

I've always loved and remembered those and many other stories, Maw used to say, 'Those were the days.'

I was told once that my father was a hardworking man with fourteen kids. I don't think there was ever enough money. My brother George told me that when I was a baby, he used to take me out in the pram to the coal yard to steal some coal. There were always other kids doing the same thing. Prams in those days had a very deep body and it was possible to take the support piece out and fill the body with coal. He said the police were constantly chasing them but very few ever got caught, probably because they felt sorry for them.

When we lived in Glasgow everyone had a butt and ben (room and kitchen), no one owned a washing machine but instead went to the steam laundry referred to by the locals as 'the steamie.'. I was tiny for my age and looked like a wee schoolgirl.

Bridie took me to the steamie one day to show me the ropes, she was a big strapping woman and when she rolled her sleeves up, she had a pair of boxers arms. When I saw the size of the sinks I said, 'Bridie, I'll never reach them to do the washing or be able to use the scrubbing board.'

She pulled two wooden boards together for me to stand on and then left me.

In turn, I'd left Bev outside sitting on the steps to watch the old pram – everybody did the same with their prams, we were right next door to a sweet shop. If Bev wandered, I knew where to find her. She'd be in that shop, sitting on top of the bags of coal and giving out sweets to the other kids.

It came to light because I used to get tick and ended up with an unexpected bill. I found out that she was telling the shopkeeper that, 'Her mammy had told her to get four penny bags of sweets and her mam said it would be okay.'

Pawn stories and more ...

We couldn't afford new clothes and would go to the Barras or Briggate where people took bundles of shoes or clothes to sell, straight off the ground, wrapped in an old shawls for coppers. We did, however, buy new bedding sets but me and maw, and Bridie would send them to the pawn. Bridie would always stress, 'Remember to get a Whitney Blanket, they were expensive blankets of pastel shades with a thick satin border at the top – I wonder if anyone remembers them? I desperately wanted one but never ever got one.

When things got pawned, they hardly ever got lifted out and usually the ticket was sold on. I think that's one of the reasons we moved so much as we were reliant on the tick man all the time who we never paid back.

I was sent to the pawn shop one day and was pregnant at the time. I used to wear stiletto heels and loved them, even when I was pregnant. While at the pawn shop, I fainted so it took longer than needed, they had me sitting on the steps outside. Bridie turned up and managed to get me home. The first thing ma maw said was 'It's because of those stupid shoes you wear,' not taking into account that I was pregnant or hadn't eaten anything.

Another time George had come to visit us in Argylle Street in Glasgow. George was always immaculately dressed, he loved good fashionable expensive clothes. We had a bed settee that he slept on while George was telling us funny stories, which he always did and was forever making us laugh. He told us stories before Billy Connolly told them.

George's clothes were hanging over the chair and were soon bundled up. I was the one sent to the pawn shop with them. I was told over and over to make tea and rolls for George and keep him telling his stories by asking for another one – but he needed to go to the toilet and kept asking for his clothes. Ma maw said 'Look son, I've had to borrow your clothes for the pawn, I'll get them back on Monday before you go home, just put that coat on and go to the toilet. It was a woman's long fur coat and he had to sit around with it on for the whole weekend.

The next day was Sunday, the day that Briggate was open. Me and maw went along and bought George a whole new outfit for half a crown for when he went back on Monday. Maw told George she had forgotten that the pawn was closed on Mondays. He never got his clothes back, but he never complained. He would tell me 'It's Bridie that's got her like that.'

I later found out that George was getting into bother breaking into shops. Once he asked me to help him with a butcher's job, he said the butcher kept his money in the front window under a metal plate. There was a close next door, and I was to let him know if anyone appeared. There was a big metal bowl sitting on top of the plate and he couldn't reach it. He accidently put his hands in the bowl which was full of lard. He couldn't get to the money, and we had to leave when we heard some people coming. We didn't even get any meat as everything was locked away in the fridges. The headline news was *What idiot leaves his prints in the lard?* He got some stick for that caper, and it stuck with him for ages.

There was a time when I used to go for the bread rolls at midnight, they were freshly made and were great. George walked me round to the bakers one night and we watched as the baker brought out a large metal oxo box up on the counter to give me my change. We went home and after our hot rolls George went out again, of course, back to the bakers. It wasn't a shop but a small building out the back door of the houses. George broke in and lifted the box in the dark. What he didn't know was that the baker had two oxo boxes. The one George stole was full of coppers, I don't think there was even £20 in it. The only thing we could spend the money on was sweets and single cigarettes.

George could never work as he had a lung condition. He had one lung and suffered from bronchitis but always came home with a few items or a few bob, nothing big, enough to get by. Ma maw managed to acquire a new suit and experience told me it wouldn't be there long and yes; it was sold round the corner at Bargain Base where they bought and sold items. I don't know how he managed it, but he broke in and stole other items to sell. I think ma maw got £100 for the suit.

George was always everyone's favourite; he was a great and very funny guy and managed to get us out of a few scrapes. He had the gift of the gab telling sob stories. He married Margaret and went on to have two sons George and Paul. Sadly, George died about ten years ago and I still miss him very much.

My daughter Ali passed away 25 years ago – she often told me that I should write a book of my life. I decided to try it so went to Social Services to ask for sight of my records from when I was in care. I had never fully understood why we were in care and fostered out, being moved from pillar to post.

Reading my social work records

I made an appointment with the manager; I knew the meeting would need more time than usually allocated because I was aware I wouldn't be allowed to take away the original records. He sat with me to discuss everything in the records, he also warned me that there might be information in there that I might find upsetting. I told him I'd be okay, then he excused himself on the pretext of making a phone call and left me alone to read my records.

The information was a bit shocking, but I managed to hold it together, all the answers I needed were there and from that I was able to figure things out but there was still a lack of information. About twenty minutes later the manager came back, he asked if I was okay, did it help answer some of my questions? I told him it had helped but not entirely. He was very kind and said that if I needed any more help to just get back in touch with him. He gave me a copy of mine, Frankie's and Louise's records up to the age of fourteen and a half – the time where we finally left care and went back to our mother.

After that I started going to the local library to try and find some old newspaper dates and names because in our records was the story of Sylvia. Our father had died the year before we went into care, Frankie being born on the same day he died. A year later Maw met someone else, Maw did know him, he was a guy who came round the streets with a horse and cart selling fruit and veg. I don't remember him, but my sister Gussie has a vague recollection of seeing him the once.

It turned out that they were married then and when he was visiting my maw, kids were stealing what was on the cart. What was revealed in the records was that maw and the plum man as we nicknamed him, were having a baby together. Then maw had a terrible shock when she found out that he was already married with five or six children of his own. He lived in Glasgow with his family and the police were looking for him because he had committed bigamy. He was eventually found and jailed for a year. Maw went on to have the baby which she named Sylvia and three months later he was released from prison. Maw later found out that he was living in a half-way house, so she went to see him with Sylvia and left her with him.

Sometime before this maw had spent time in jail – I think it was for breaking into the gas meter and stealing ten shillings. She probably needed money to feed us. Somehow the papers got hold of the story, according to George, they sent round a photographer who captured a picture of us, I was the baby in the picture. We were all sitting round the table eating porridge. The headline in the next day's news read: *Children eating porridge while mother does porridge.*

I'm still trying to track down the paper that ran the story. I believe it was the building that held all the paper records went up in flames in the 1950's and its possible that this record was destroyed in it. However, I will keep looking.

After Sylvia's birth and the shock of the bigamy my mother was really struggling and finding it hard to cope with everything. She couldn't pay her rent and was being evicted – I believe that was when we were taken into care because of neglect.

I never knew anything about my grandparents and was told years later that they had disowned ma maw. I never found out the reason why but was told they were very strict Catholics. By all accounts my grandmother had several sisters and she worked as a housekeeper in St Mirren's Chapel in Paisley. They were also quite well off. She owned some properties in the area as did her sisters, so I don't know why they didn't help. Perhaps it was because she went to prison or maybe because she had married a bigamist but knowing me, I'll keep digging.

Bridie stayed with our gran for a short while but was sent back home because she stole from her and was getting into trouble because she stole some people's Monday books (pension books). For that she was sent to a home called 'The Good Shepherd – for girls who couldn't be controlled at home.' Gussie also went to stay with our grandmother and loved it.

They bought her lovely clothes, and she was well looked after; Gussie was always well behaved and nicely spoken – years later we thought she was a bit of a snob – she never got into trouble.

When I got my records, I showed her ours and she wanted sight of her own. I got Gussies for her and when we looked, we noted that all the stories that were written had virtually the same information – as if one had been copied four times. But at least we had access now to all the full stories and secrets.

I was later told that my mother was in prison when her mother died. She was allowed out to go to the funeral. It must have been a terrible experience; especially given they never spoke. Most of my older family have died so I can't ask them anything. There's only Bridie, but she won't say anything. There are more revelations, but I don't want to say too much as I don't want to hurt anyone. But one day, I will say.

CHAPTER 18

Sylvia

We weren't getting all the answers fast enough about Sylvia. My kids kept at me to keep trying; they were keen to find out what happened to her. Bev and I found dates and names to start with. Bev is more adept with the computer than I and found a lot more information very quickly.

Then one night I received a call from Bev, 'Mam, are you sitting down? We've got some good news for you. We've found Sylvia!'

I was frozen to the spot and couldn't believe what I had just heard. I burst out crying, Oh my God it was a strange feeling, I really didn't believe that day would happen.

Bev's first information was that Sylvia had married in Paisley and both she and her husband worked there. She also had two children but sadly one had been involved in a tragic accident after the family had moved to live in London. By all accounts the child had fallen out of a tree and died.

Bev spoke to the remaining child, Gayle, first. We weren't sure whether Gayle wanted to meet up at first but when Bev explained why she was looking Gayle burst into tears and said her mother, Sylvia would be over the moon. She told Bev that Sylvia had also been trying to find her family for years.

We made arrangements to phone each other, Gayle told us that her mother was very quietly spoken and a bit shy.

Bev reassured her saying, 'Don't worry, my mother isn't.'

We were all excited, but Sylvia didn't phone as arranged. Gayle told Bev to ask me to call her the next day at 7pm.

The first thing I said to break the ice was, 'What time do you call this?'

We laughed about it years later. We must have spoken for three hours, and Bev and Gayle connected over Facebook and communicated all the time from then on.

Gayle was living in Peterborough and went to London to visit her mum and dad, so we all decided to meet up. In fact, we took it one step further and planned for a reunion involving my kids and her family.

A couple of years earlier, after I had been diagnosed with breast cancer my friend Lesley suggested I should get in touch with the Breast Cancer Care Team who, along with the Record paper, put on a charity event every year at The Hilton Hotel in Glasgow.

Everyone dressed in different style clothes and appeared on stage modelling all the different fashions. It was a lovely and fun experience, and we stayed over for a night so we would be ready for our rehearsals.

We had guests who paid for their own tables; twelve to a table and each person paying £150 each. It was for a good cause, my guests were Bev, Tina, Bren, Michelle, Sonia, Lesley, Louise, Lorraine, Sarah, Janice, Sarah-Jane and Jennifer. I would have loved Catherine, Corina and Ciaran there, but I thought it may have been too upsetting.

We had a lovely meal and drinks, and everyone was dressed up to the hilt in their gorgeous evening gowns and jewellery, the men too looked handsome in their evening suits.

Libby McCarthy from River City was the host for the evening – there had been an afternoon show too, hosted by Halla Mohiddeen. We all had an escort from the Scottish Rugby Team who walked us individually on to the stage. It was wonderful, we felt like a million dollars and were told to just enjoy and strut your stuff – which I did, no change there. Everyone cheered loudly and made us feel so special.

I met some lovely people who had had the same thing – it bonded us, I'll never forget that experience, also I got to tell each one our own story. I told Ali's story, of when her medallion was stolen and how she had died some twenty years earlier with breast cancer and the follow up to my own diagnosis.

After dinner we then joined our own guests and then the auction began. Bren's employers Loake Bros Shoe Factory kindly donated a beautiful pair of shoes and raised a lot of money. Also, my son in law donated a beautiful shoe cleaning kit made of mahogany, that was special, my friend bought it and donated the money to the cause. What with that and the money raised by people paying for their place at the table I was so proud of everyone who supported me and the charity on that special night. We were told if we wanted to do a show another year, we could but because of Covid, it hasn't returned – myself and the family will be giving our support when it does.

Our family have had fund raising events in the past and raised about £4,000 and happy to do it.

The Reunion

So, we started the arrangements for the reunion. It was during covid, and we were just coming out of lockdown which meant there were limitations as to where we could book. A lot of the family wanted to be involved.

We looked at a lot of venues such as the Glynhill Hotel, but they couldn't do the food. We wanted a buffet but that wasn't possible because of distancing restrictions. Eventually we found somewhere else.

Bev and Gayle stayed in touch and because we wanted it to be a surprise, Sylvia wasn't told. We secured a date for July having booked a place with a lovely beer garden; it was ideal for our purposes.

I had a huge banner with 'Welcome Sylvia to your family' made and ordered a limo to pick her up and a piper to pipe her coming out of the car. Sylvia's husband Stewart, his sister Lilian and her family were all in on the secret, even the limo picking Sylvia up from Lilian's in Linwood. She had no idea.

The limo picked her up at 5pm and took her for an hour's drive. I'd instructed the driver to take her to her old address where she was brought up, showing her where I was born and where she lived when she was fostered then on to Todholm Terrace in Hunterhill, Paisley.

After all our conversations a few coincidences that popped up, like when me and Louise were fostered out at Beech Avenue. It was just five minutes from Todholm Terrace which we weren't aware of. At the time all the kids would go down to the school during the weekend evenings. It was directly across the road from where Sylvia lived with her foster parents and two stepsisters.

The schools she went to, when she left school and where she started work - Bev had found all this information out. She started work at fifteen at the Brown and Polson factory but left after a year. I knew someone who worked there who recalled a young lass being there and not stopping for long.

I found out that she worked at the Co-op but didn't know exactly what she did. It was a huge shop with a restaurant at the top; a very smart tearoom. She had met a young man called Tony and they got engaged and wanted to emigrate to Canada or New Zealand, Tony suggested he went first, get a job and house and then Sylvia could join him but Sylvia didn't want that and so they split up. This was all in my records.

So, when we played at the school at the weekends in the evenings, we had made friends with some other kids. Sylvia told me of an event where she had brought a friend home, probably to use the toilet and her foster mother asked the wee friend what's your mummy's name. The wee girl answered Mary McKenna then they went back out to play. When Sylvia returned home that evening, she was told that she couldn't play with that wee girl again. There was no explanation given only that 'she's from that home up the road,' we worked out it was either me or Louise. A few days later the Welfare came to visit us and we were moved to another care home 'Barrholm' in Largs. We weren't told why until Sylvia realised that Mary McKenna was also her mother because she was named Sylvia

McKenna Hillhouse Gordon, Gordon being her foster parents name and Hillhouse being her father's name.

Bridie always maintained that Sylvia was adopted – but that was not the case. Bev had sent Gayle photos of myself and all the family. These were passed on to Sylvia. In one of them there was a photo of me wearing a headscarf as a band around my head, in fact it's my Facebook picture taken after my breast cancer scare. My hair was starting to grow, and I wore all these scarfs. Sylvia recognised me as that wee woman at the bingo one night when she came to Scotland to visit Stewart's sister. They went to the Globe Bingo in Johnstone on a Tuesday night and happened to sit opposite me and asked me to sort out their books.

Sylvia remembered us because I used to sit after the bingo and have a drink and sing-along. I told Sylvia if I'd heard someone calling her name that night I would have said 'Oh, I'm looking for my sister, she has the same name as you,' There weren't many women about by that name and it may have come out sooner.

I got in touch with the reporter who did the story about the breast cancer event as they wanted to cover the story. They sent along a photographer to take pictures of all the family he also took pictures of Sylvia and her family too. Capturing that event at the beer gardens and Sylvia stepping out of the limo at the reception with everyone crying with joy and standing cheering was wonderful. I recall we could hardly walk the response was so overwhelming.

My sisters Bridie and Gussie and my brother Eric were all waiting to meet her – sadly they were the only siblings left. Eric passed recently and I managed to go to visit him in Fort William when he died. Eric and Sylvia spoke every week after the reunion and really bonded. She said she was glad that she met him before he passed. He wanted to be buried back in England near to Kettering. Sylvia and Stewart came to the funeral – it was nice to see them but sad because of the occasion. We went for a drink and a meal afterwards and had a good catchup and arranged to meet up on their next trip to Paisley which I think will be in March. We are all looking forward to that.

After the reunion

Gayle has since moved to Scotland and is staying with Lilian who hasn't been keeping too good and is waiting to go into hospital. They came to Scotland last Christmas, and we all went for a meal. It was a great night, something to really cheer us particularly having lost Louise the previous year. She had developed dementia after retiring from her job of 53 years, but then she caught covid and died in hospital. She had always wanted to find Sylvia.

I miss Louise terribly; we were very close. She was so fit, she walked everywhere and to end up with dementia was heart-breaking – and losing Frankie - all we had been through together, and myself to still be here to tell our stories, both sad and happy memories. So, now there are only 4 sisters still here, Gussie was very ill last year but getting better slowly.

Bridie is currently in a convalescence home and going into a care home soon. She's ninety now and needs assistance and help. I speak to her every day on the phone and try to visit as much as possible. Gussie is hoping to get up to Scotland in March with her daughter Joan because we intend to lay some flowers at the mass grave found about eight years ago of some four hundred bodies of children who died while in Smyllum orphanage. Some of the bodies date back to a couple of hundred years ago. Some of the reasons for the deaths were made up because some of the deaths were because of horrific abuse.

When the story broke, I got in touch with the Sunday Post reporter and told them that one of the bodies found may have been the child that my sister found dead in his cot one day. I phoned Gussie and asked what the name of the little boy was, the one who had died that time. All she could recall was the name David. The reporter arranged for me to lay a huge floral arrangement at the graveside, for all the children who had lost their lives at Smyllum – the story went global.

About a week later I had a phone call from the same reporter asking me if I could speak to David's elder sister Jean. He passed on my number to her, and we had a chat. She wanted to hear all about David, especially Gussie being the last person to hold him. Apparently, none of the family was ever told or knew what had happened. She desperately wanted to meet Gussie, I said I would try but then Covid happened, and Gussie went into hospital and was very ill there for six months. Thankfully she is picking up now. We've phoned each other a couple of times since and tried to arrange a get together with Gussie, Joan, my kids, Sylvia and Jean to put flowers at the graveside but unfortunately our brother passed away and

Gussie wasn't well enough to travel. We are hoping that this year in March it will happen. I've bought a couple of nice planters and bulbs and flowers with brass plaques on them to put at the memorial stone erected in their names. We all hope we can do it.

CHAPTER 19

A few wee stories

I was given a painting for my 65th birthday from my niece June and her family. It was Vettriano's 'The Singing Butler'. There was something familiar about his paintings and I realised it reminded me of a time when I was living in Largs (at Barrholm Children's Home). My favourite charge hand was a lady called Mary Kirkwood. She would come to work on Saturdays all dressed up. After work she headed for the afternoon ballroom dancing matinee. She was a fabulous dancer and taught me the basics of the jive – but Mary did it properly, the ballroom way. Rock and Roll had just started so we watched the American way or, as we called it, the Glesga jive to the Six Five Special pop show that was on the tele. I admired Mary so much. She was perfect, lovely make up and a great figure and during the week her hair was in a bun or a ponytail, but most Saturdays it was beautifully set like the 40's or 50's era. So, the lady dancing on the beach reminded me of her. I love that painting and still have it hanging in my living room, it's a lovely memory of Mary Kirkwood.

Mussels

I also thought I'd share another wee story with you all. I recently had a flare up of Crohns Disease and the doctor arranged for me to have bowel screen. I received an appointment two weeks later and had to go on a low fibre diet the week before. My appointment was for the Tuesday so on the Saturday I treated myself to a bag of garlic mussels – boil in the bag in their shells. I could have any number of fish I wanted which I love. I settled down Saturday night to watch Ant and Dec and had just started to eat the mussels. I had my fourth one ready to eat and turning to the tele, put it in my mouth without realising a piece of the shell was still attached to it. I swallowed and too late, it got lodged in my throat. I tried to bring it up, but nothing happened.

My niece Nikki would have been my first call, but she was on a night out. I didn't know if I could speak so I phoned my daughter Bev in England thinking she'll know what to do. Somehow, I managed to tell her that I needed to go to hospital. She called Nikki who was with me in minutes, took me to the hospital, explained what had happened then her sister Donna and her friend Irene came up to keep me company.

I was sent for x-rays; they could see it was lodged but couldn't remove it. I was told I would have to go to the Queen Elizabeth Hospital. It left me boaking, trying to bring it up. I said to the Doctor perhaps if I had a piece of bread and water, that might shift it. We tried and nothing happened. So, I was sent up to Glasgow, somehow it didn't feel as comfortable as it had been.

I was given another x-ray, only this time the doctor said she couldn't see anything – which was good. I explained about the bread which she thought might have moved it into my stomach, but my throat was still sore and swollen and it felt like it was still there. The doctor told me that I had badly torn my throat and gullet and I would have swelling and be sore for a few days.

I was in bed for 10 days, never ate a thing, just sips of water and ice cubes and milk. All I thought about was, 'well, at least I'll lose a few pounds,' I couldn't even speak. Everyone was saying, that'll keep her quiet for a while and give us a break, joking of course.

Nikki and my other niece Anne and nephew Thomas were great and so helpful. Thank you.

I was in the house for seven weeks altogether because I had to have my appointment at the hospital for my bowel screening (colonoscopy). They couldn't do it because I was too ill, so they scheduled another appointment. That appointment was cancelled because my flare up had got worse and was too painful. I was put on a four-week course of steroids and told to wait for the next appointment.

Fortunately, my flare up is settling down and my throat is a lot better, so I'd like to take this opportunity to say to everyone, after two months of running to the toilet every 10 minutes, thank you.

Yesterday, I was like a wean. I always check my bowel movements and I had a normal poo. I shouted out loud, 'YES, a normal poo! Can you believe how relieved I felt. So please everyone, check your poo, it's very important. And check your breasts and finally, check your mussels in shells please. Health check alert.

CHAPTER 20

Onwards

I am being supported by a team called Future Pathways who help and support survivors of abuse while in the care of these homes. They are helping the survivors get their rightful compensation awarded by the government.

I am grateful to Future Pathways for all their help, support and guidance. They organised help for me to get support with writing my book, from a writing coach called Lea at The Book Whisperers. We get together each week to write this book which I enjoy very much. Sometimes I get quite upset with some of the things and must stop writing for a few days.

Even when we were searching for Sylvia, we applied to Long Lost Family, but Bev found her before they got in touch – which they never did.

I also helped Eric with his application against Smyllum, he suffered terrible abuse while in there by nuns called The Sisters of Charity, what a joke. After Eric died, I stayed with his wife Maureen, for another ten days – they had already arranged to move back to Kettering, Bev had helped Eric with this because she knew how unwell he was and that this was what he wanted before he died. Sadly, Eric didn't make it, even though a house was found, and Bev and Future Pathways had paid for the removals and the first month's deposit. They helped so much.

I moved with Maureen and her family members who were so kind and supported her. Her sister, who lived in Corby, near Kettering was unwell and in hospital at the time and unfortunately, a couple of months after the move, she passed away.

I stayed with Maureen for another couple of weeks to organise her moving in. Everyone helped. Thomas, my nephew was the only one from Paisley who stayed in touch and kept an eye on my house. His Mum, June, passed away last year. June was not only my sister Ella's daughter, but she was my niece and my friend. She was always there for me and a good listener. She only lived four doors away – sometimes I would arrive at her and Tam's house where we would sit for hours. I know Tam could be a pain in the backside sometimes, but I loved June, she could never do enough for me or anyone else and she always looked after my house when I was away.

I have had a full and eventful life and have been blessed with the love and support of family and friends. I have always tried to find fun in life, or perhaps it has tried to find me, either way, life is too short not to smile and it doesn't cost much to make people laugh and be happy.

Live each day as if it were your last and make sure you leave people thinking of you with a smile on their face, 'Let me see you smile. If I can make you smile, I'm happy.'

I'm a survivor, not a victim.

ACKNOWLEDGEMENTS

Thank you ...

To all my children, Bev, Tina, Ali, Bren and Simon, for all their love and understanding and the full support they have given me from the very start and for never judging me on anything.

Also, my nieces Nicki and Anne for all the hours you spent on the computer – thank you.

My daughter Bev gets a special thank you for helping with recollections, finding Sylvia and all the administrations.

To friends and family for allowing me to tell their stories in my book, in particular my sister Louise and brother Frankie – we started out this journey together, but sadly they are no longer with us.

My husband Roy, who asked my mother for my hand in marriage along with four tins of salmon and £10 digs money.

To Future Pathways for helping me with In-care Abuse Redress Scheme, for the financial advice, support, understanding and help in starting me off on my writing path by introducing me to The Book Whisperers who helped me write my story – I am so grateful to you all.

To my newfound friend, Lea Taylor from The Book Whisperers.

It is very much appreciated and thank you all.

And lastly,
My Mother
'Maw'
Mary McKenna

A NATURE ADVENTURE

By Josie Drage-Dawes

Lizzy Rice, Geordie Rice and Davey Bryce, all lived in the seaside town of Largs, Ayrshire. They all attended St Mary's school in Largs and because it was spring, their teachers asked everyone to go on a nature trail that weekend and write up an essay ready for the following Monday. They asked them to write about animals, specifically the new-born spring arrivals and as many flowers which were in bloom that could be found. They asked for as many specimens and drawings as possible. Everyone was excited as they loved a nature study.

After school on Friday, Geordie, Lizzy and wee Davey couldn't stop chattering and wondering where to go. But Friday was always fish supper for tea, so they raced home to go to the chippy.

As they left their mam shouted after them 'Don't forget, extra vinegar! And don't forget to collect wee Davey's order from his mam.'

They collected wee Davey's mam's order every week without fail. Davey's mam and their mam were sisters. Their mam was called Loulou and Davey's was called Daisy.

They went out to play for a while and talked about where to go for the nature trail on Sunday. Eventually they decided to go and play down the glen. The glen was new to wee Davey, he had never been there before but still got excited at the prospect of going there.

Lizzie and Geordie had a big Alsatian dog called Bruce and wee Davey had a Jack Russell called Jock, the two dogs went everywhere together.

The next day, the Saturday, the three of them went up the High Street for Mam's shopping after breakfast – which was usually porridge or cornflakes and toast - while their Mam wrote out her shopping list and Lizzy took her mam's wee trolley. Geordie got his wee geig (go-kart) out to help carry the shopping home then round to Wee Davey's to collect their aunty Daisy's shopping list.

Off they went, dogs on their leads. They stopped at Mr Lamb the butcher's first for mince, a square slice, steak pie, links, ham ribs for soup and the same for aunty Daisy. Next to the butchers was the fish monger and dairy run by Mr and Mrs Spratt. Two kippers and 6 fish fingers each and then on to Mr Pastry the baker for 6 scotch pies, half a dozen mixed cakes each a dark crust loaf and a pan loaf for the pieces for Sunday. Plus, 6 well fired rolls each - thank you Mr Pastry. They needed to go back to the dairy for ½ lb bacon and two ½ lb pats of butter. And lastly came Spud Murphy's the greengrocer. They wanted two lots of everything please, carrots, cabbages, onions, a bag of mix fruit and two bags of mixed broth. And that was the lot.

Then they piled it all into the geig, and Lizzy's shopping trolley to take back home. Meanwhile, outside the shop Bruce and Jock started barking frantically outside the butchers.

Alerting the children to the fact that they had forgotten to get them bones from the butcher. Geordie was quick to go back in and Mr Lamb handed him some bones.

Lizzie's mum's name was Louise, and they all called her Loulou, and their Dad's name was Geordie, Wee Davey's mum was our mum's sister, and his dad was called Frankie – they nicknamed him Funky as he was so funny. Our dad and Davey's dad both worked on the buses.

After delivering all their shopping home they got their pocket money and off they went to the bike shop where you could hire a bike for 4 hours – which was something they did every Saturday. The dogs weren't allowed to go with them when they went on their bikes, so Lizzie suggested they went to Haile Brae. It was a very steep hill and not many kids went there – as not many managed to even get halfway up. So, they walked up as far as they could, holding the bikes and when they had got so far, they would jump onto the bikes without peddling and whizz down the hill. It felt like they were flying. But poor wee Davey couldn't do it because of his wee legs. Lizzy said, 'You wait at the bottom of the hill and watch.'

He watched with bated breath and thought it was exciting, screaming with laughter when Lizzie finally came down. She said, 'You never mind Davey, maybe you can do it next year when your wee legs grow.' Then he turned and shouted to Geordie and said 'I can't wait until next year Geordie cause Lizzie said my legs might have grown by then and I'll be able to fly down the Haile Brae'

Lizzie and Geordie went up the brae one more time and then they rode off to the Pencil down by the sea front. It's a big monument in the shape of a pencil. Lizzie said it goes way back to the Viking times where a lot of battles were fought. Lizzy is very clever as she goes to the library all the time.

Geordie and wee Davey announced they were hungry and suggested going to the chippy for a big poke a' chips wrapped in a cone shaped newspaper filled with chips 'with extra vinegar on them please.' They loved Zavaroni's chippy and they sat at the pier watching the steamers coming and going to the different islands of Millport, Rothsay and Arran.

Wee Davey piped up 'Geordie, what do you want to do when you grow up?' and he looked at Wee Davey then back out to the sea.

'I want to steer one of those steamers, and what about you Wee Davey?'

Wee Davey's face brightened, 'I want to be a train driver,' then he looked at Lizzie, 'And how about you what do you want to do?'

'I want to be a vet and work in the library part time.'

Then Wee Davey piped up, 'I knew you were going to say that Lizzie because you go to the library all the time.' Then he jumped up off his seat and said, 'Let's go down on the beach and collect some shells and pebbles.'

But as it turned out, they had to take the bikes back first. They were delighted to each be given a threepenny bit back for taking such good care of the bikes. With that they knew they could buy an ice-cream pokey hat with raspberry squirted on it.

Then they noticed a crowd of kids on the beach looking at something, curious they stepped closer to see what the commotion was only to find it was a porpoise, a huge marine mammal rather like a dolphin. It was dead with its stomach ripped open. They knew how it happened, had seen it before. The porpoises chase after the steamers and get too close.

They all helped roll the poor creature back into the water and then headed home, stopping off to buy a pokey hat from Nardini's Café. They walked home, quietly licking their cones.

They had a quiet night in watching our favourite cartoons and films and then off to bed. The next morning, they woke early and had a wash and their mam made their breakfast of lovely, fired rolls and a square slice with brown sauce. This was their usual Sunday breakfast.

After breakfast, their mam started doing our pieces with water and not forgetting Jock and Bruce's treats. Then off they went to meet up with Wee Davey and Jock. It was a lovely spring day and they had to walk about thirty minutes before coming to the glen.

There was a few people out and about walking their dogs, going for morning papers and seeing the milkman delivering his milk and eggs. At last, they arrived, shouting with delight, letting Jock and Bruce off their leads to race into the Glen. With their bags on their backs, they raced after them, Lizzie took up the lead and spontaneously started to sing:

I love to go a wandering along the mountain track.
And as I go I love to sing
With a nap sack on my back
Fal-de-ree, fal-de-rah, Fal-de-ree, fal-de-rah, ha ha ha
With a nap sack on my back.

All of them all singing at the top of our voices. The first thing they noticed was all the beautiful spring flowers, thousands of bluebells, daffodils, crocus, buttercups and daisies. Lizzie would patiently tell them all their names. She was clever, she explained that they were only allowed to pick a couple of bluebells each as they are a protected plant and if everybody took bunches home there wouldn't be many left for others to admire. She said the rest was okay but just to pick three of each and to put them in the little plastic bags for our essay on Monday morning. Then Lizzie asked Wee Davey if he wanted her to show him how to make a daisy chain to take home for his mam as a necklace cause his mam's name was Daisy.

'Is my mam named after a flower?'

'Yes,'

'Are you called after a flower?'

'Yes, I'm named after a bizzie lizzie.'

'Is that why you are always going to the library?'

'Yes, I think so Davey.'

The two dogs were still happily running about chasing each other. Having spotted some buttercups, Geordie shouted 'Lizzie, show Wee Davey how you can tell if he likes butter.'

Lizzie turned to Wee Davey, 'Okay pick a buttercup and put it under Geordie's chin. What colour does it show? Wee Davey picked up the buttercup with his little chubby hands and held it under Geordie's chin. His eyes widened, 'Yellow,' he whispers, 'does that mean he likes butter?

'Yes, now pick another one and put it under my chin. What colour is it Davey?

'Yes,' squeaked Wee Davey. 'You like butter too. Me next, see if I love butter!'

Lizzie reached down and carefully picked a buttercup and held it up to Wee Davey's chin. He held his breath with excitement. 'Yes Davey, yellow. You love butter. Now, put the flowers into your plastic bags and remember to write them up in your jotters.

Geordie was drawn to a croaking noise he heard at the side of the fence.

It was frog. Geordie was beside himself with excitement and called Wee Davey and Lizzie over to see.

'Sshhh,' whispered Lizzie, 'you'll frighten it away.'

So, they just sat for a while then Geordie piped up, 'Can I name the wee frog Lizzie, cause I saw it first.'

'Yes,' Lizzie nodded.

Geordie thought quietly for a minute then whispered 'I know what I'll call him, Freddie. Freddie the frog.'

'Yes,' Wee Davey agreed.

Freddie the frog croaked another couple of times and then jumped into the water.

Geordie paused to write about it in his jotter and then they began picking all the different flowers whilst at the same time listening to the wood pigeons coo-cooing high up in the trees. They couldn't really see them as they were perched so high up.

Suddenly, Bruce and Jock started barking at something in the shrubs. Wee Davey ran over to investigate. Excitedly he waved his arms beckoning Lizzie over, 'Look, we've found a hedgehog, come and see it. Let me give it a name, please. Please Lizzie.'

'Okay, but let's say hello first.'

They hunkered down and looked.

Then Wee Davey began jumping up and down with excitement. 'I know what his name is going to be, Ozzie. Yes, Oggi my best friend at school his cat died, and his name was Moggi Oggi so now my new friend is called Ozzie the Hedgehog. Can we sit for a while Lizzie?'

Lizzie nodded thoughtfully then whispered, 'But only for a short while because while we sit here Ozzie won't move and can't go look for food for his family. Wee Davey understood and waved cheerio to his new friend.

Then Lizzie realised that a little robin had been following them twittering away. She pointed it out to Geordie and Wee Davey who said to Lizzie that they thought robins only came about in winter to which Lizzie explained that the older robins hang about to make sure that none of the last ones got lost.

'So, what are we calling him?' Geordie and Wee Davey chorused. Lizzie turned on the brightest of smiles and said, 'I think I'll call him Rockin Robin,' and they all burst into song, singing the Rockin Robin song.

Then Bruce and Jock barked again and began pulling at Wee Davey's back-pack and they realised they were all hungry. 'Yes,' said Lizzie, 'We'll have something to eat,' and even Rockin Robin went tweet, tweet, tweet as if he was saying it too.

Geordie threw some crumbs down for him and soon there were loads of birds gathering round while they sat and ate their pieces. When they looked about them, they noticed that the grass was full of tiny little purple flowers called a forget-me-nots.

Lizzie asked the boys, 'Do you know why it gets the name forget-me-not? They shook their heads. 'Well,' Lizzie started to say, 'When you come to a place like the glen, and you see all the lovely trees, flowers and animals, you won't forget them and write their names in your jotter.'

Wee Davey said, 'I'm going to write everything in my jotter because I don't want to forget anything about today. Thank you, Lizzie and Geordie, for bringing me to the glen and I might learn everything like Lizzie because she loves to go to the library.'

Then they got up and began making tracks home. They got to a part of the glen where it was a bit more open with fields on each side. The first field was a corn field with a big scarecrow standing in the middle. Wee Davey asked what it was for, and Lizzie explained when a farmer ploughs the fields and plants the seeds, all the blackbirds fly down and peck them up. So having a scarecrow standing in the field makes the birds think it's a person and they stay away.

'Look,' said Lizzie, pointing to the two big horses pulling the plough guided by two farm hands. 'One of those horses is a Clydesdale horse and the other is a Shire horse, they are very strong.

The farm hands saw the children watching them and started guiding the horses towards them.

'The dogs have to go on their leads.' Geordie shouted to Lizzie. The horses came close to the fence where they shook their heads and neighed and nodded. The children were so excited and happy, then the farm hands docked their caps, waved and shouted, 'Cheerio – have a nice day.'

To which the children jumped and danced with delight.

Across the other side of the glen was another field with cows and their new-born calves. Geordie shot a look at Lizzie and said, 'Lizzie, you didn't tell us the horses names.'

Lizzie smiled and said, 'I was so excited I forgot but I know what their names are. They are Bonnie and Clyde – oor mam and dad loved a film and song by that name. They'll be over the moon. Bye Bonnie and Clyde, we'll see you another day.'

Off they went and at one end of the field of cows they saw some sheep with their lambs. Wee Davey shouted 'I want to call the sheep over there in the corner with their lambs Molly and Dolly. Is that okay Lizzie?'

'Yes Davey,' said Lizzie. 'Those are good names.'

As if approving, the sheep called back, 'Baaa.'

'What about the cow and the calf, shall we name on each Geordie? I'm going to call mine Buttercup,' And Geordie said, 'I'll call mine Daisy after Wee Davey's mum, Aunty Daisy.

Wee Davey clapped his hands with delight, and they all shouted out together, 'Write it in your jotter.'

Then Lizzie suggested they went to the farmhouse to visit Farmer Giles and his wife.

Wee Davey hadn't been to a farm before, and his face lit up with a smile. 'That's a good idea Lizzie.'

And they all burst into song, Old Macdonald had a farm, ee i ee i, ooh.

As they got nearer to the farm Lizzie saw Mrs Giles hanging out her washing. 'Hello,' she shouted, 'Isn't it a lovely spring day.'

Mrs Giles called back 'Yes children, it is.'

Then Farmer Giles came out to greet them and they said, 'This is Wee Davey, he's our cousin and is eight and a half.'

Farmer Giles nodded and then said, 'Our wee pig Bella has had her piglets, eight of them. Come and have a look.

Wee Davey asked, 'Did you call her Bella because she has a bell on her neck?'

'Yes,' said Farmer Giles.

They watched the piglets trying to fight each other for a feed, then they heard clip clop sounds coming from the back yard and walking with a sheepdog called Buddie were two old donkeys.

The children walked over to them and noticed that they were indeed very old. Farmer Giles explained that they are retired now and live happily at the farm content and no longer working at the beach giving rides to the children.

'What's their names?' piped up Wee Davey.

Farmer Giles gave him an indulgent smile and said 'Ally Bally.'

'Oh, that's lovely names, aren't they Davey?'

Davey nodded and beamed back at Lizzie. 'Can I feed them?' he asked.

Farmer Giles handed them each a carrot.

Davey was happy then he said, 'Farmer Giles can I work on your farm when I grow up and when my legs grow bigger?'

Farmer Giles laughed and said, 'Of course you can. Children should learn about nature and farm animals at a young age. The earlier the better.'

Then Wee Davey leaned forward and whispered into the donkey's ears 'I'm coming to look after you soon.'

The donkeys nodded their heads and brayed.

Mrs Giles appeared from the kitchen with a big pot of tea and a plate piled with sandwiches.

The children smacked their lips whilst they were watching two bengal cats lying in the sun – one named Duchess and other named Henrik.

Then Lizzie noticed a big dandelion and said to Wee Davey, 'If you blow on it, it will tell you the time. So, see how many times it takes for you to blow everything off. It will know what time it is. One, two, three, four. Its four o'clock. Time for us to head home.'

'That was really clever Lizzie,' said Wee Davey, 'Wait till I tell mum and dad I can tell the time with a dandelion.'

They waved and shouted their goodbyes to Farmer Giles and his wife and promised to return another day and thanked them for a lovely day.

Off they went down the glen, but Farmer Giles shouted Geordie back and Mrs Giles handed him two egg box cartons with six large free-range eggs for their mothers as a gift.

'Thank you, Mrs Giles, our mums will be very happy with them,' said the children and they waved goodbye again.

'Remember to write everything in your jotter,' called Mrs Giles and the children laughed and waved.

Geordie spotted Rockin Robin following them again, tweet tweeting away. All the animals were leaving the fields one by one with Buddy the sheepdog rounding up all the sheep and their wee lambs following.

The children waved and shouted cheerio to them. What a wonderful adventure day they'd had, and they couldn't wait to get home and tell their Mam and Dad and school on Monday. They looked back at the glen, and it was full of little rabbits running all over the place.

'I think we'll try and bring a camera with us next time we go to the glen,' said Lizzie, 'because I want to show yous the secret hideout.'

Printed in Great Britain
by Amazon